BREAD PUDDING

AND OTHER MEMORIES:
A Boyhood on the Farm

EDWARD J. RIELLY

LITTLE CREEK PRESS™
A DIVISION OF KRISTIN MITCHELL DESIGN, LLC

Mineral Point, Wisconsin USA

Table of Contents

Acknowledgments

I gratefully acknowledge the publications in which the poems and a few of the prose entries in this memoir previously appeared, in some cases in slightly different form and with a slightly different title:

The Breaking of Glass Horses and Other Poems, by Edward J. Rielly (Great Elm P, 1988):
> "A Constant Pace"
> "A Way of Ending"

Good Old Days (August 2002):
> "Threshing: The Perfect Way to Spend a Hot Summer Day"

Good Old Days (September 2003):
> "My One-Room Schoolhouse"

Growing Up With Baseball: How We Loved and Played the Game, edited Gary Land (U of Nebraska P, 2004):
> "Just Me and the Barn"
> "Playing My Cards Right"

Hard Row to Hoe (Spring 2005):
> "The Man with One Good Arm"

Magnapoets (January 2011):
> "Why My Mother Wouldn't Drive"

Ways of Looking: Poems of the Farm, by Edward J. Rielly (Moon Pie P, 2005):
> "Climbing a Pine Tree"
> "Gathering Immortality"
> "Hands Reaching"

These pages are dedicated to the people who live within them,
and who live in my memories and in every day of my life: my parents,
my sister, my brothers. I also dedicate this memoir to those who entered
my life later: my wife, Jeanne; my children, Brendan and Brigid; their
spouses, Erica and Phil; and my grandchildren, Morgan,
Shannon, Maura, Sadie, and Molly.

Introduction

I hope that this memoir brings enjoyment to its readers. I also hope that it helps readers learn more about a way of life that has largely disappeared from the American scene. Schools have changed. Farms have changed. Ways of working and playing, along with ways of living, have changed as well. The life that I lived as a child in rural America has passed away and will not return. However, I believe that this way of life deserves to remain alive in the collective memory of the nation and in the consciousness of individuals who never had the opportunity to experience this way of life. And I do mean "opportunity," for it was in many ways a wonderful way of life.

I look back on my childhood with deep gratitude: for my parents, who were enormously hardworking and who gave me far more than money (which was always in short supply), especially their consistent love and concern for my welfare; for the rest of my family; and for the supporting cast who helped populate my school, the surrounding farms, and my hometown. I am also enormously grateful for those who have entered my life in later years, starting with my wife. It is for both sets of people that I have most of all written this account of my childhood: to honor the first and to help the latter know me and my life a little better.

I made several choices in writing this memoir. First, I decided to focus almost exclusively on my childhood, generally cutting off my reminiscences around the time I entered high school. There are a few exceptions as I occasionally look toward the present, but mainly I stay with that part of my life that I believe holds the most interest for people not immediately connected with me. I find the rest of my life personally very interesting, but I am not so sure that most people would share that interest. My childhood, though, coming, as I said, from a past that is almost totally past, is a different story—in more ways than one.

One of the challenges in writing this memoir was to decide how to structure it. I settled on a lot of moments that highlight important aspects of my childhood rather than a chronological narrative because that is the way I remember my life. I would argue as well that I lived my life that way—in moments. Young children, like most adults, typically do not experience their lives in rigidly constructed plot narratives.

I have placed my moments under major headings that relate to significant aspects of my youth. Some overlapping inevitably occurs in the incidents that I recall, and some of the individual entries could well have been placed elsewhere in this book. On the whole, though, I leave it to the reader to read this memoir as he or she wishes: either from the beginning straight through to the end or by dropping in here and there.

I.
Harvesting and Other Farm Matters

Threshing: The Perfect Way to Spend a Hot Summer Day

Threshing was one of the highlights of the year when I was growing up in the early 1950s on a dairy farm in southwestern Wisconsin, right up there with Christmas, my birthday, and the last day of school. Looking back and realizing how hard the job was, I have to wonder about my sanity during my youth, but I always looked forward to the annual event. And not because of the huge community meals, the table loaded with meats and potatoes and pies and cakes, and not the camaraderie among neighbors—those things about threshing that appealed to the grown-ups.

What I liked so much were three aspects of threshing, one of which occurred before threshing day, one during it, and one afterward. In short, I really looked forward to shocking, shoveling oats, and sliding down the straw pile. Let me tell you what appealed to me about each.

For those of you not familiar with the various stages of threshing, which in essence is the process of separating grain from straw, in our case oats from straw, a few words about this business may be in order. First, someone had to cut the oats with a binder, which not only cut the oats but also gathered it (still on the stems, or straw) into bundles and dropped the bundles onto the field of stubble. A tractor pulled the binder, and a common pattern consisted of my sister driving the tractor with my dad on the binder seat. Then people had to stack up those bundles into shocks, which looked like golden tents, for drying. This was where I came in.

My brothers and I shocked, that is, we constructed the shocks, usually eight bundles to a shock, although that may have been just a regional variation on a theme. Four bundles faced one way, and four faced them, all leaning inward to support each other, so a small tent-like opening led into the shock. It was hot, often steamy work, necessitating durable work gloves and a hat to block the sun. There was a real sense of artistry to it, though, yielding a beautiful field of shocks at the end of the day.

Edward J. Rielly

By the way, those bundles of oats are sometimes called sheaves, but the famous hymn notwithstanding, I never once heard anyone in my family or any of our neighbors call them that.

Mary and I prepare for a good slide down the straw pile.

Within a few days came the threshing itself. Neighbors arrived in the morning after milking, as the neighborhood migrated from farm to farm, following the threshing machine that one of our entrepreneurial neighbors owned. The shocks had to be forked up onto wagons and hauled to the field where the threshing machine had been set up to accept the bundles. Bundles went onto a conveyor belt to be pulled inside the bowels of the machine where oats and straw were separated, the oats collected while the straw was blown out through a long high pipe. The straw gradually formed a hill known lovingly as the straw pile.

Here is when my second favorite part of threshing began. The oats were released through a chute into the box of a truck and hauled into the barn. I would grab the wide grain shovel (in other settings it might be called a coal shovel—if there is a difference I'm not sure what it might be) and crawl into the back of the truck. My sneaker-clad feet would sink into the golden grain, oats finding their way not only inside my shoes but even inside my socks, the oats more tickling than annoying.

It was not so much the shoveling that I enjoyed, that hard and heavy throwing of grain into the oats bin, the oats landing on the rising hill within the bin, some sliding back down, the rest adding to the hill's height, but the grasshoppers that kept leaping about. They shot off my legs like mini-rockets at a Fourth of July fireworks display. How those grasshoppers fascinated me! When I finished unloading and looked into the bin, the oats seemed completely alive with the bursting energy of those little creatures. That energy, of course, would soon die out, the grasshoppers' brief lifespan ended, and when I opened the door to the bin a day or two later, the oats lay strangely inert. Even the gold was hidden within the shadows of the bin. Only when I dipped out a handful of the grain and stepped to the barn door, holding the grain out into the sunlight, did I see the richness of the harvest filtering through my fingers.

After the threshing came the final reward for me. Despite my mother's warnings about children falling through and suffocating amid the straw, I delighted in climbing the straw pile, seldom an easy task. I would lose traction and slide backward, landing on a soft cushion of straw ringing the pile. Often, though, I managed to claw my way to the top. There I would sit, gazing about at the farm, the meadows and corn fields stretching out around me, and resting in the welcoming depression my body made. Finally I would step to the edge, sit down, and slide groundward. It was not, I must admit, a particularly fast slide, nothing like sledding on an ice-slicked hill, but it was fun. From my subjective point of view, that straw pile was, following the cutting and binding and shocking and hauling and separating and shoveling, what the whole process was there for. It was why threshing had been invented, not to provide the oats to feed cows or the straw to make life softer for them on a winter's night. I slid down, I now know, looking back these many years, with great joy but toward a future called adulthood.

That's not a bad future. It has lots of joys and some sorrows. But it does not have any golden shocks, millions of grasshoppers exploding at my feet, or tall, soft mountains of straw for a boy to climb and slide down and climb again. It would be nice if it did, but it does not.

Those Threshing Feasts

I'm afraid that I gave short shrift to threshing dinners when I talked about threshing. It is high time to undo that mistake, right that wrong, or maybe I am just hungry at the moment. In any case, let's go back to those days. Everything that I said still stands. All of the aspects

Edward J. Rielly

of threshing that I said meant a lot to me still do. But then there also were the dinners.

And they were dinners, though held at noon. Growing up on the farm, meals were clearly articulated: breakfast was in the morning, dinner at noon, supper in the evening. Now, living in a less rural area, we experience breakfast, lunch, and dinner. The term "supper" is rarely used, and something called brunch has cropped up, although it remains somewhat rare, not an everyday occurrence. On the farm, we would not have had time to break for brunch, as it would have seriously interrupted our work patterns.

We had a lot of folks to feed on those days when the neighbors were threshing on our farm, farmers from most of the farms in close proximity to ours, at least those who raised oats, and that was virtually everyone. Feeding so many men took a lot of women to prepare the meal, and how they prepared it! Several meats, mountains of potatoes, baskets of buns, vegetables, and, most importantly, dessert. Dessert meant pies: apple pies, cherry pies, butterscotch pies (one of my mother's specialties), chocolate pudding pies, rhubarb pies. Pie after pie after pie. If a farm wife could not bake anything else, for sure she could bake a pie.

It stands to reason that all the farmers, working out in the fields, came in mighty hungry but also mighty covered in dust and straw, with oats falling out of their cuffs. Washing up took place at a hydrant between our driveway and the yard. The water was cold, but on a hot day that cold water felt good: a lot of lather on the arms, a lot of splashing, cold water dripping from the face.

Then came the meal. In order to accommodate everyone at once, it helped to have some picnic tables, always, of course, under trees. Something about growing up on a farm put sun in perspective. Lying around in the sun is fine for city folks who don't get much of it, but when you spend most of the day riding a tractor or forking shocks into a wagon, or otherwise accumulating a high dosage of sun, shade is what you want.

As a young child, before I became old enough to help with the threshing, it was a lot of fun to watch the men wash up and see the bounty of the feast and observe the heaping plates of food. Seconds seemed mandatory, and no one said no to a piece of pie. Calories, well, probably no one even knew what a calorie meant or, if so informed, could have cared less. Of course, I definitely got my own piece of pie.

Later I became one of those washing up as well. Maybe the meal was even more enjoyable then, when I had worked harder to earn it, although choosing between two superlatives—two versions of the most elaborate and tasty meals ever—is hard.

Cleaning the Barn

When I grew old enough to hoist a pitchfork full of heavy, dripping cow manure, I inherited the job of cleaning the barn. Lacking an automated barn cleaner, that type of mechanical contraption that scraped the manure slowly down the gutters (channels cut into the floor) toward the door and up a short chute to plop into the manure spreader, I had to perform the task manually.

I never cared much for the task—not because it was heavy work or boring work or even dirty work. I didn't so much mind getting my hands dirty, or my clothes, but I sure hated what happened all too often on windy days.

I can still taste the experience now, literally: fork loaded with heavy, dripping manure, my arms swinging back, propelling the fork forward, the manure flying off through the door into the spreader—and then the wind! A gust of wind lying in wait until that split second after my arms had reached the point of no return on their rush forward. The wind slapping manure back in my face.

Under the circumstances, there was not much for me to do except wipe off my face with the back of my shirtsleeve and get back to work. Maybe a strong spit or two. It was clearly a battle I could not win. No one outthinks the wind, devilish imp that it is.

Still, one can look on the bright side. Getting an occasional face full of cow manure prepares one for almost anything in later life. If you get my drift.

Edward J. Rielly

Katie and Sam

We raised sheep on our farm. Actually, I raised sheep. Town kids got part-time jobs bagging groceries or pumping gas. I raised sheep. It generally was not a difficult job. Sheep are not high maintenance most of the time. Of course, the money was not as regular as a grocery store paycheck.

Mainly I earned my money once a year when we sheared the sheep. We hired a traveling shearer who amazed me with his ability to sheer a sheep in what seemed like about two minutes and end up with one sheet of wool, no hacked pieces, no frayed fragments. Then he rolled the wool into a ball and tied it with twine. After the shearing, my dad and I loaded the balls of wool into the back of our pickup and took them into town to sell. Dad backed up the truck to the loading (and unloading) dock, and we unloaded the wool. At that point, only the weighing of the wool stood between my paycheck and me.

But when I remember my sheep, in addition to the shearing, I especially think of Katie and Sam. One of my ewes died after giving birth to twins, one female, one male. I named the twins Katie and Sam after an aunt and uncle. I always loved visiting Aunt Katie and Uncle Sam when we went into town. She always insisted that we not leave without eating.

So regardless of the time, day or night, we ate, even if we had just arisen from a big meal. Each lunch was the same, but always delightful, I must add. It grew steadily. Aunt Katie always said that we would have "just a bite." So we sat around the kitchen table, and she got some cheese out of the refrigerator and set down a plate of crackers. Then she added a platter of cookies. But she periodically would return to the refrigerator to retrieve something more, some luncheon meat, some leftovers from the day before. The bite kept growing.

But what really stood out were the sugar cookies. The best sugar cookies I have ever eaten. No one ever made sugar cookies the way Aunt Katie made them. Like my mother's frycakes, which I talk about elsewhere in these reflections, the ultimate, once experienced, stays with

Grandfather McKeon sits for a photograph surrounded by his surviving children. Mom is behind his right shoulder; Aunt Katie is to the left on the top level.

you over the years, and every other version—of cookies, doughnuts, whatever—pales in comparison.

I had to feed my lambs by hand, using old 7-Up bottles with rubber nipples on them. I used cow's milk but added a little Karo syrup so the milk would agree with the lambs' stomachs. The lambs were quick learners, and as soon as they saw me approaching the fence they rushed to stick their heads through, their little mouths open. They loved that milk, slurping and smacking their lips, tails swinging madly left and right. Patience was not an attribute they possessed, so I used two bottles, neither one inclined to wait for his or her turn.

The only problem with all of this was that I never thought to mention to my Aunt Katie and Uncle Sam that I had named two lambs after them, an oversight that proved embarrassing one Sunday afternoon. After Mass, we brought my aunt and uncle home with us for dinner. It was a nice day, the sun shining brightly, few clouds in the sky, my two twin lambs cavorting happily in the pasture.

So as we drove along the gravel road just prior to pulling into our

Edward J. Rielly

driveway, I, without thinking, yelled out, "Hey, there's Katie and Sam!"

Silence descended, and bewilderment filled up our car. And then I explained. It was all right, of course, but maybe I should have told them earlier. Not everyone understands how a boy's mind works when it comes to bestowing honor: favorite aunt and uncle, beloved lambs. It makes sense. At least it did to me.

Poor Sam—the lamb, not the uncle—did not live to a ripe age, but Katie (both Katies, actually) did. Even throughout adulthood, Katie would trot over to me whenever I entered her pasture. She gave birth to several sets of her own lambs over the years.

Since, of course, I stopped giving her milk laced with Karo syrup when she grew up, she had to find other treats. That led to a serious problem one day. As she was reaching toward some succulent leaves on a tree, with her front legs leaning against the trunk, one leg slipped and landed in the crook between branches and broke.

We put Katie in the back of the pickup, and Dad drove us to town. Down Main Street we went, Katie bawling in the back, my dad probably a bit embarrassed, on our way to the veterinarian. Katie recovered, although her leg remained bent. She always hobbled a little, but her fondness for me continued. I reciprocate that fondness yet—toward both Katies.

Barn Fire

Much that was wonderful happened when I was growing up on that dairy farm. There also were funny events, a lot of hard work, and more than one moment of tedium. There was also, occasionally, something really terrible, and for a farmer not much is worse than having his barn burn down, especially with livestock in it.

That occurred to a farm family who lived north of us. He was one of our closest neighbors, although several fields and fences, plus a cow lane and some woods and hills, intervened.

One night a fire broke out in their barn. The fire rose high into the sky, a horrifying sight. There is nothing pretty about a barn fire. The fire trucks came, of course, but it took a while for the trucks to cover a dozen miles, especially when the firefighters were volunteers and they had to drop whatever they were doing, wherever they were, to rush to the fire.

In truth, there was no way to save a barn in those days unless somebody saw the fire when it had just started. The most one could hope for would be to save the other buildings and perhaps rescue some of the cattle, and the latter only if a lot of luck came into play.

My father rushed there to see if he could help. For the rest of us, as we gathered on a ridge beyond our backyard, we all knew what we were watching. Even a young child could understand. I understood. I had spent enough time observing my father's fondness for our cows, listening to my parents worry about making enough money to pay the bills, seeing the hard work involved in filling our barns with hay and oats, to understand our neighbors' loss.

There's not much more to say. Neighbors pitched in afterward, naturally. People can help with rebuilding. Wives can bring food. The farmer can buy replacement cattle if he has decent insurance, but those cows are not the same.

Years later, when I was away living my postfarm life, the barn on the farm belonging to my sister and her husband burned down. Cattle died. Grain and hay turned to black masses. The silo attached to the barn still stood but was damaged beyond repair. They never rebuilt. They never milked cows again. I never asked why, but I understood then even better than I had years earlier that replacing can be as heavy emotionally as financially. Sometimes one just has to move on.

Edward J. Rielly

Making Cheese

That cheese factory down the road, just close enough so that I could make out the roof from the front porch of our house, was the destination of our milk for quite a few years before I was born and during the first few years afterward. The Evans family—father and sons—ran the cheese factory in the basement of the building that also served as their home, the top story looking much like a house, but the first story unmistakably a factory. They made what we called American cheese. Today that name is seldom used except in Wisconsin. Its variants are Colby, cheddar, and Monterey Jack, names far more likely to appear on supermarket packages today.

My father and older brothers—Lawrence and Joe—would haul the milk to the cheese factory in the morning after milking, using the tall milk cans that held, as I recall, about ten gallons of milk. Those cans were heavy—really heavy—when they were full of milk. The cans had to be sealed tightly so that no milk would spill out into the box of the pickup en route to the cheese factory and so that nothing would get into the milk, which was strained of physical impurities when we poured the milk into the cans in the milk house. We continued using those cans long after we no longer hauled milk to the cheese factory, a milk truck instead picking them up, so I had plenty of years to grow accustomed to them.

In the milk house, which was attached to the barn, a strainer sat on top of the can, and the milk followed the path from cow to milking machine to milk pail to strainer to milk can. The strainer pad had to be replaced several times during each milking as the pads collected pieces of straw, dirt, or any other nonmilk particles.

The lids were designed to fit snugly and be tough to knock loose once on, which also made them hard to remove. The lid had a wide, heavy lip running around its circumference. The tried and true method of loosening the lid was to bang upward under the lip with the edge of another lid.

We had to keep the cans cold, especially those from the previous night's milking, which we initially did in a tank of cold water and then, after we built a milk house attached to but separated from the barn by a thick wall, in an electrically powered box cooler. Those cans were heavy to swing up and into the cooler, a task my father or older brothers would handle. The cooler contained very cold water, so as long as we did not lose electricity the milk was in no danger of spoiling.

My father and brothers would come back from the cheese factory with whey, a watery byproduct of cheese making. Disposing of whey could potentially be a major problem for cheese makers if they were forced to haul it away for dumping, so they were happy that farmers found a use for it: feeding it to their pigs. Pigs, after all, will eat just about anything, and whey is nourishing enough. This use of whey proved to be a win-win situation for cheese makers and farmers, as it also helped to cut down on the expense of feeding pigs. Today whey is used in a lot of products, such as bakery glazes, low-fat soups, and, in a dried and concentrated form, in various bakery products, including cakes and muffins. Maybe we have more in common with pigs than one might have thought.

Eventually, big cheese makers began to push out the little ones, and they had their own trucks to haul milk. The Evans cheese factory closed, although the family continued to live there, and our milk cans went off to a bigger plant. We later switched to a bulk tank, which eliminated the need for cans. We never did modernize enough to have the milk going directly from the milking machines through pipes to the cooler. We (often I) would carry the milk pail to the strainer and pour the milk through the strainer that now sat atop a round hole in the top of the bulk tank rather than on a milk can. No more lifting of the milk cans, which was a great advance. My back thanks the person who first invented the bulk cooler, for by the time that I became old enough to hoist those heavy milk cans we had switched to the new cooler.

Edward J. Rielly

Eating Cheese

I love cheese. I love it so much that I don't even need to add an exclamation point after that first sentence. That growing hunger I feel as I just think about cheese is exclamation enough. People in (and from) Wisconsin deserve the nickname "Cheese heads"—at least many of them do, not just because Wisconsin is the cheese-making capital of the country but also because—and this is directly related to the prevalence of cheese in the state—so many Wisconsinites enjoy the yellow stuff.

Of course, not all of it is yellow. That qualification especially refers to my favorite cheese—Limburger. Limburger, which can be almost white, is the cheese that leads most people not from Wisconsin (and many even within the state) to hold their noses and groan. I do admit that it can give off a heady aroma, one that remains attached to fingers, knives, plates, counters, and anything else with which it comes into contact. Wrapping it multiple times in plastic bags, aluminum foil, or similar materials helps to keep the interior of a refrigerator less odiferous after that block of Limburger has been sliced into.

But how I love Limburger! There, I had to get in an exclamation mark even if I didn't need it. I learned to appreciate Limburger from my dad, who also taught me how to eat it: sliced not too thin and placed between two Saltines. Limburger is best when middlingly soft—definitely not hard, but preferably hard enough to retain its sliced shape with just a little drooping.

The main problem with Limburger is that because I no longer live in Wisconsin it is hard to come by. Wisconsin, as all cheese aficionados know, is a prime producer of that particular cheese. However, it stands up well to mailing so long as the seller packs it well, meaning that it stays cold. Of course, one can find Limburger imported from Europe, especially from Germany (the name coming from the Duchy of Limburg, which is now part of Belgium), but that is not the same and hardly deserves mentioning. No cheese measures up to Wisconsin cheese.

So what other Wisconsin cheeses have I especially enjoyed eating? Swiss, of course, although the Swiss cheese experience has changed from when I was a child. Then we would stop into the cheese factory or cheese store and be given a taste (a nice thin slice) from a large wheel of Swiss cheese. Those wheels could be as big as three feet across. Then a fat triangle of cheese would be cut off the wheel and wrapped up. We would keep our Swiss cool, but it was usually best not refrigerated if possible. Hot days, though, would make it too rubbery, so refrigeration might prove necessary, with a little time outside of the refrigerator before eating. Aged Swiss was—and remains—my favorite version of Swiss. Aged cheese has more bite to it than mild, newer cheese, more of a lasting aftertaste, like a good glass of wine.

American cheese (Colby, cheddar) is fine, but to my taste less distinctive than Limburger and aged Swiss. It works well, however, in grilled cheese, my favorite sandwich (what else?).

Then there is brick cheese, a kind many people outside of Wisconsin have never heard of. Brick is a bit like a very, very mild Limburger in consistency and color. It has more of an odor than most cheeses but less than Limburger. Brick apparently got its name from the brick-shaped loaves in which it was made. According to Jerry Apps, in his enormously informative book *Cheese: The Making of a Wisconsin Tradition*, John Jossi, a cheese maker in Dodge County, Wisconsin, first made brick cheese in the 1870s. Brick entered the world of Wisconsin cheese about a decade after Limburger was first made in the state.

So there we are, all set for a mid-afternoon snack. Grab your crackers and cheese and get to it.

Chickens and Ducks

All the farmers in our community raised chickens, if not for sale, then at least to provide eggs for their own use. Ducks were less common but hardly rare. On most of the farms, ducks just wandered around, living out their uncertain life spans, their fate subject to a marauding fox or a large rubber tire. Few farmers around actually ate ducks, except once in a great while, perhaps on Christmas.

We were mainstream regarding chickens and ducks. For a time, my mother raised chickens for sale. We bought the baby chicks in large, square cardboard boxes, heavily perforated so the chicks could breathe. The day we brought home the boxes of cheeping chicks was one of the highlights of the year for me. Knowing all the work involved in raising those chickens—the feeding, the watering, the cleaning of the brooder house, as we called it (the chicken house being for the fully grown hens)—my mother was less thrilled. She also was the person who did most of the killing and cleaning of the chickens just before they reached adulthood, when the meat was still tender. Still, she looked forward to the money for those almost-grown chickens.

But for me, there was great excitement when the boxes arrived, so full of noise. I would help my mother carry the boxes out to the brooder house and empty them, lifting the chicks out gently. We had the feeders full and the overhead warming light on so the chicks, so newly hatched, would not take a chill.

Of course, I also had to pitch in with the chicks, especially with the feeding. They were smart enough to learn quickly, milling around my feet as I stepped gingerly, generally sliding my feet so as not to step on any of them. Once in a great while, despite my best efforts, I would fail. The sound of a chick squishing underneath your shoe is about the worst sound imaginable.

I have to admit that I did not care at all for the killing of those chickens. I tried not to watch. It was bad enough to see them soaking wet after my mother had dipped their dead bodies in boiling water to loosen the feathers, which came out more easily then.

The ducks brought more unadulterated pleasure. We never killed them. In fact, we did not do much of anything with them. They were not really pets, because we never played with them. I'm not sure what games one could play with ducks. But I enjoyed watching them, especially the young. The ducklings would follow, waddle actually, after their mother. Those were times to watch from a distance, as the mother could get pretty upset if she feared her babies were in danger.

Like the male of many animals, the drake was best given very wide latitude. He might just as likely take a run at me as anything. It happened often enough to keep me on my guard.

How many times have people, speaking of rainy weather, said, "It's great weather for ducks!"? Little do they know. Rain, especially a heavy downpour, is exactly not what ducks want, especially if they are very young and have not yet developed their rainproof feathers. Many times after a heavy dunking, we would go out searching for the newly born ducklings and find some in bad shape: soaked, battered, and extremely cold. Sometimes, one would even be dead.

We would bring the soaked ducklings, those still alive, into the house to try to save them. The best place for them was on the linoleum floor right in front of the kitchen stove. We would lay them on a towel on the floor. Then, when they started to come to, we would try to feed them a little. Some small pieces of soft white bread soaked in water worked the best.

Some of the rain-soaked ducklings died, but we saved a lot over the years, happily returning them, very carefully, to their mistrustful mothers.

The big drawback of the ducks was that they were not clean animals. Putting it tactfully, they did their bathroom stuff rather forcefully, depositing quite a bit behind. And it was rather messy stuff. For that reason, we tried to keep the ducks out of the yard and especially off our porches. They usually complied.

Back to chickens. After we stopped raising chickens to sell—the business becoming too much for my mother, and my father and brothers busy enough with the rest of the farm work—we still kept hens for eggs. We gathered most, but the hens hatched enough to keep the chicken house populated with an ongoing line of egg producers.

Most of the time, the hens were not a problem. They spent their days scratching in dirt for treats in addition to the grain we would feed them. The rooster, of course, had to be watched. He had a tendency, even more often than the drake, to put his head down and take a run at my legs.

In the evening, the hens slept on the roost we constructed in the chicken house, an apparatus consisting of a grid of slats. Chickens on the ground are easy prey for invading critters. It was funny how they

Edward J. Rielly

slept, the head tucked underneath a wing. Maybe the morning sun bothered them.

But gathering eggs could be a challenge. Hens are often loath to give up their creations, perhaps thinking of all the little chickens they are losing. Those hens often would stay right there in their nests, a series of boxes a couple feet off the ground. That meant I would have to stick my hand right in and feel under the hen for an egg. The hen, as might be expected, tended to take offense, and too often would retaliate with a sharp poke of her beak. Now a beak poke is not likely to cost a hand or arm, not even a finger, but it can hurt. And although most of the time the hen does not actually attack, especially as I got good at quickly sliding my hand underneath, grabbing, and yanking, there was always that fear of danger. I offer a poem about the experience:

Gathering Immortality

Gathering eggs I discovered early to be
something between art and war, sliding
my hand slowly under the chicken

where the egg might be, if she
had carried out her proper function.
It was always guesswork, feeling

among the bristling feathers
and the softly scratching straw
for the brittle touch of the shell

hidden in the wooden box open
to the front and high enough to keep
the possums out. The hen would strike

with a short downward motion,
pull back and strike again, thinking,
perhaps, of future generations lost

and chicken immortality. Or merely asserting
ownership rights in the face of my hostile
takeover. Whatever, my hand, numb with fear

at ten, jerked back, my head darting
shadows beneath the nighttime roost
of intersecting slats barely two inches wide,

where, above the earth, my hens would roost
beyond all earthly concerns, twisting
heads under their white wings
to dream of eggs as things inviolable.

The Outhouse

Memories of our outhouse remain vivid for me, reinforced by the
power of the tactile sense, especially on cold winter days. The
outhouse as a name is a strange combination of the literal and the figura-
tive. It certainly stood outside, but to call it a house is stretching things a
bit. A house is someplace to seek shelter and comfort from the elements,
an edifice in which we achieve security, where we long to be. No one
to my knowledge ever longed to be in an outhouse, either during the
biting cold of winter or the fly-buzzing heat of summer. Nor, for that
matter, at any time in between those extremes, as there was just no way
to avoid the odorous assault of the outhouse.

Yet it was something of a tiny house. It had four walls, a roof, and a
door. Ours had no window, although others sometimes did. There was a
seat, although hardly one of comfort—far from an easy rocking chair, a
plush recliner, or even a good, dependable kitchen chair. Just a wooden
bench with two holes in it. The reason for two holes always escaped me.
Given the absence of any partition, visiting the outhouse was not a community exercise, at least in my family.

I came along, though, after definite technological improvements to the nature of an outhouse. Old Sears and Montgomery Ward catalogs had given way to rolls of soft toilet paper, which meant a certain degree of enhanced comfort.

The outhouse had another, far less genteel, name: the backhouse. Now that name may have derived from the practice of constructing the outhouse in back of the main house, but, truth be told, it may also have had a more vulgar origin best left to the silent imagination of readers.

A child always had the fear of falling in. That no one I knew actually did so never completely eliminated that fear. The pull of gravity could be felt in a bit of slippage now and again, just often enough to keep the user of the outhouse on his or her toes, so to speak. A more immediate danger lay in dropping something down one of the holes, which consigned the dropped object to eternal loss. No one in his right mind would even think about attempting a rescue—for reasons too obvious to sink into at this moment.

Honesty is important, of course, and honesty requires an admission here that in the most brutal winter weather we sometimes took the easy, at least the warm, way out. Yes, we used a chamber pot. However, we never called it that. It was just the pot. Always, naturally, kept well covered and hidden away out of sight. And, also naturally, often emptied with a quick dash to the outhouse.

Also at my one-room Fort Defiance School we used outhouses. There we had two, one for boys, one for girls. Constructed at opposite ends of the playground, they were designed to keep the sexes as far apart as humanly possible while remaining firmly rooted to school property. In winter, there was no indoor alternative. At twenty degrees below zero, we still had to head to the outhouse, where shivering mightily, we wasted no time getting the job done and hurrying back to the welcoming warmth of the old oil stove in the rear of the school.

Years later, I attended an outdoor arts festival hosted by a couple on their small farm, which consisted of a few acres and a large garden. They were wearing overalls untouched by hay dust or cow manure. In addition, they had constructed an outhouse, a real one, but it seemed primarily for show as they also had a real bathroom in their house.

Whether they actually used the outhouse was unclear to me. Given a choice, one would be a fool not to choose indoor comfort instead. Having experienced outhouses when I did not have much of a choice, I would not willingly choose one.

It was with great joy that we finally installed a bathroom in our house, complete with a bathtub, a shower, a sink, and, best of all, a toilet. I remember the innovation vividly, as I remember the outhouse vividly. A trade for the ages, no matter what someone playing farmer might think.

Blizzards

Winter in southwestern Wisconsin was fun much of the time when I was growing up, although it was seldom so for my father. I would race downhill grasping my wooden sled, smash the metal runners onto the snow, and flop belly first on the wooden slats, enjoying the rush of wind as I roared down the slope. There also were plenty of other games I played in the snow, at home and at school, but all of that I leave for anther time. Here I want to talk about blizzards.

As I said, my father had little joy in winter. His tasks inevitably proved more difficult as he tried to maneuver through biting wind, falling temperatures, and rising snow. I remember well his lying on the snow-packed ground to drape chains over the pickup's tires. When the snow rose too deep for a tractor to maneuver through it, manure piled up outside the barn doors waiting for a thaw so it could be hacked from its frozen mounds and hauled away to be spread in fields—free fertilizer moneywise but expensive enough in effort. The stock tank, which stood in the barnyard and provided water for our cows, froze over daily, and since we lacked any way to water the cows within the barn, we had to let them out for a drink. That meant chopping away the ice in the stock tank with an ax so the cows could get at the water. These and many more trials and tribulations of winter made farming an even harder business. Yet worst of all were the blizzards.

Edward J. Rielly

For a child, a blizzard had its advantages—no school being the most important. But for my dad, a blizzard just made everything worse. Start with the water. The blistering cold tended to freeze our outside hydrants, which meant that no water would be available for watering the cattle and sheep. Nor was there water for mixing up what we called the slop—powdered feed mixed with water—for the pigs. Unfreezing hydrants was necessary but challenging. Boiling water sometimes worked. Of course, it did not take long for boiling water hauled from the house, where the indoor pipes had a better chance of remaining open, to lose its boiling.

The most likely hydrant to remain available was the one rising directly out of the concrete underground pump room. Unfortunately, the pump room was right outside the gate leading from the lawn to the barn. We had to carry buckets of water from there across the driveway to the barnyard to fill the stock tank if we could not get the hydrant near the barnyard gate to work. Not a bad job if all we had to do was carry a bucket or two on a nice day, but a challenge in biting weather when many buckets would be necessary to satisfy all the cows.

Occasionally, not often, but on the other hand even occasionally was too often, the water also froze inside our house. Then we had to rely on that pump room hydrant also for our household needs: for drinking, washing, and, after we got our bathroom to replace the old outhouse, flushing. Carrying buckets of water could become almost a daylong job. Carrying them upstairs to the bathroom definitely was no fun.

All of this proved very inconvenient at best, a severe economic loss at worst. Such was the case when the roads became so filled with snow that the snowplow was delayed getting through and our milk tank in the milk house filled with milk.

Then no remedy remained except to use as much milk as possible: feeding it to the pigs, making some butter, and so forth. But that accounted for only a little of it. The rest had to be dumped or it would go sour. Dumping milk was like taking your paycheck to the bank, cashing it, and then building a bonfire in your backyard and tossing the money in. There is no replacement for cash, and there was no replacement for the milk. In fact, dumping the milk was even worse than the bonfire option. At least that would produce some warmth.

The milk truck came daily, shortly after morning milking, to remove the milk. We could go a second day if necessary, but after that we ran out of cans or, later, tank space. The road crew understood the situation well and made every effort to open roads, knowing that the farmers' livelihood depended on the milk truck getting through. Yet they could do only so much. When Mother Nature gets angry enough, no one stands in her way.

One winter it snowed and snowed. That blizzard seemed to know no bounds. The snow piled up, and the snow plows came through again and again, but eventually there was no place to put the snow.

We had to dump our milk. It was a terrible situation. My parents had little enough money, certainly not enough to waste. And dumping milk was such a physical, concrete example of waste. It was, as the saying goes, enough to make a grown man cry.

Finally, the township came through. The roads still were incapable of being plowed, but a bulldozer was enlisted to move from farm to farm through fields. The road plowing had helped for a while but then became counterproductive. The snow pushed to the sides had packed and become so hard and heavy that plowing would not work until all snowing stopped and a little sun softened the snow a bit. But in the fields, where there had been no plowing, the snow had not packed that way, and the bizarre effects of natural blowing and drifting meant that a careful journey through a field could occur where the snow was not too deep.

So the bulldozer made its slow way through the fields, with the milk truck right behind it. Fences had to go, but replacing some barbed wire was a happy expense for being able to ship the milk off for processing— and for a paycheck. It took a long time, but the little procession finally arrived. It was quite a day when the bulldozer came through.

Another blizzard-induced experience stands out in my memory. I was in high school. The snow started after the school buses had deposited all of us at school, but the snowstorm quickly expanded into a blizzard. School officials retrieved the buses and sent us on our way, hoping that everyone could get home before the roads became impassable. Not everyone made it. Those who did not had two choices: ride back into

Edward J. Rielly

town with the buses, a decision that might lead to several hours stuck in a ditch waiting for someone to haul the bus free, or get off at the last stop.

I chose the latter. Bobby Carey was older and, for that reason, we were not close friends. But he was a nice boy, and he invited me to stay with him and his family. So I departed the bus, which started its difficult journey back to town.

I stayed with Bobby and his family that day and, if I recall correctly, all of the next day. His parents were very gracious, and I had a good time. It was something of an adventure to be marooned in a blizzard, although I could hardly have been marooned more comfortably.

Spending a night someplace else in those days was an uncommon event for most farm kids. Although I sometimes stayed overnight with an aunt and uncle in town when I had a late play practice during high school, I never slept over at a friend's house the way children today do. The reason may have been that most farm children had their own chores and were expected to do them. Also, farm kids lived a good distance away from even their closest friends, and parents were far less free then than today to jump in the car and deposit a son or daughter somewhere. This was my first, and final, sleep-over during my growing-up days if one does not count nights spent with relatives.

On the third day of my marooning, with many of the roads still un-plowed, my mother called with a plan. I would start walking home and my brother Joey would start walking toward me. My mother tended to worry and did not want her youngest hiking several miles alone in weather that, although now clear, remained cold, and with a lot of snow still filling in the roads.

So I set off and eventually met up with Joey, who was thirteen years older than I. While many people called him Joe, I always, then and later, called him Joey.

I imagine that my brother was not crazy about the assignment, but come for me he did. I have no memory of what we talked about on the way home. Actions speak louder than words anyway, and the actions, in this case my brother's rescue of me, have stayed with me, and always will.

Snowplows and Road Graders

Snowplows and road graders were common sights on the gravel road that ran in front of our house. We had rough winters in Wisconsin, a subject that I talked about just a moment ago, especially in connection with our distaste for blizzards and the hardships that they could induce. Actually, the term "snowplow" may need a little clarifying here. It could be a heavy plow attached to the front of a truck strong enough to bull through several feet of snow. Or it could be that same road grader that we would see in summer, this time pushing snow rather than gravel.

For those unfamiliar with road graders, the vehicle had a long, thin body, which became increasingly thin toward the front. It had four large tires toward the back and two smaller tires at the front end. The front tires could rotate sharply to the right or left, making the grader flexible as the driver maneuvered it around corners and at angles. The blade, located about a third of the way back from the front tires, could be positioned to push gravel or snow straight ahead or to the left or right. The driver was exposed to the elements, so he had to be especially hardy and warmly dressed in winter.

The arrival of either vehicle was an occasion to be noted. Either it was making it possible for us to get out and others, especially that daily milk truck, to get in during winter; or it was smoothing the road in the spring and summer, a necessary function as gravel roads, which are at their base dirt roads with a layer of gravel added, are prone to develop gullies and ridges after a heavy rain, making driving on one a lot like traversing an extended washboard. No longer do people use washboards with their corrugated surfaces to rub dirt out of clothes during washing, but dirt roads capable of nearly shaking the life out of vehicles and passengers alike remain. So smoothing out the wrinkles is still a welcome activity.

We usually knew the drivers, who had a difficult job, especially in winter. Those snowplows, especially the road grader type, could get really cold. Sometimes the driver would stop in to get warmed up. My

Edward J. Rielly

mother was always happy to put on a pot of coffee for him. Since our driveway marked the dividing line between Fayette and Willow Springs townships, our farm was a logical spot for a break.

Farm culture, at least in Wisconsin in those days, dictated that no one went away from one's door without having enjoyed a cup of coffee and "a bite to eat," as folks would say, a bite typically being a lot more meal than snack. Of course, we also would get our driveway plowed out of the visit.

One of the drivers was also a close neighbor of ours. For him, my mother would make that "bite" even bigger. Unfortunately, he had a tendency to drink a bit too much at times, and I do not mean coffee. That did not occur, so far as I can recall, when he was on duty. However, I recall another time when he was just passing by, or trying to, in his pickup. He came up to the house well under the weather. That evening my mother kept the coffee pot bubbling even longer.

One of my favorite toys, as I say elsewhere when I talk a lot more about my toys, was a yellow road grader. I still have it, in almost pristine condition, with its blade rotating as well as ever. It remains one of my favorite survivors from my childhood play, and it never fails to take me back to my childhood. Another childhood road grader existed as a drawing, made by another neighbor, Nile Evans. I recall that drawing elsewhere, too, during my comments on Nile. It seems as if I cannot get away from road graders.

Lightning Storms and Tornadoes

Winter brought blizzards, and summer ushered in lightning storms and, less commonly, but often with great devastation, tornadoes. If blizzards had some compensating factors, such as a break from school, summer storms were a more unmitigated threat.

Take the typical lightning storm, for example. Midwestern storms consist of lightning, thunder, high winds, heavy rains, and sometimes hail. All of these are bad. The winds knock down crops; an especially heavy wind can leave an almost ripe oats field looking as if some giant machine had rolled through huge swaths of it. Hail can do even more damage; even the smallest balls of ice are capable of smashing crops toward the ground with more force than even a strong rainstorm and high winds.

Rain, of course, was essential. Nothing would grow without it, and streams and springs would dry up, creating problems for farmers who relied on these natural sources of water for their livestock. Yet rain at the wrong time could be harmful as well. Even a moderate rain could wreak havoc with our harvesting schedule. Just when the hay was cut and raked, waiting to be bailed, or when we had the oats shocks dry and ready for threshing, along came the rain to make everything wet, necessitating a good drying out period before we could move ahead with getting the hay or oats into our barn. If it took too much time for the hay to dry, our harvesting schedule would be thrown off. Repeated rains might make it impossible for the hay to dry completely. That could lead to hay molding before it all had been fed to the cattle. Farmers quickly develop a love-hate relationship with rain.

But, oh, those thunder and lightning storms! They really scared me. The wind that tagged along could be just as frightening. These storms seemed to come primarily at night, or maybe because they were more frightful then, I more vividly recall those storms that occurred after dark.

First came the loud, rumbling thunder that seemed to shake the roof and sometimes even the very foundation of the house. If we were lucky, the thunder stood alone, the lightning off in the distance, but too often the lightning followed right behind. It lit up the night, flickered all the lights in the house, and sometimes drove the entire house into darkness as the electrical power vanished.

Looking out of the kitchen window, I could see the dark shapes of trees against the dark sky, and watch the wind wildly waving branches in the big trees, as if they were about to break apart. The young, thin-trunked trees in our yard bent over, tops almost touching earth, appearing ready at any moment to snap off. Fortunately, none ever did.

Lightning probably affected my family more than most people because of a tragic incident that occurred prior to my birth. Several men, including my father and my brother Lawrence, were out in an oats field helping with threshing at the farm of Carroll Gordon, a neighbor. As I mention elsewhere, threshing brought the community together, the neighborhood men and women moving from farm to farm as one farm after another completed the process of separating oats from straw.

A young man named Harold Flood was on top of a load of oat shocks, the load almost ready to be pulled to the threshing machine. Dad was on a load nearby. Suddenly, out of a blue sky a bolt of lightning shot down, striking young Harold Flood and killing him. Dad was thrown off his load by the impact of the lightning strike but, fortunately, was not hurt.

My father and some of the other men put Harold Flood on the back seat of Harold's car, a car he had recently bought and that he had proudly driven, honking, past our house earlier that morning. They stopped at our farm so that my mother could accompany them to Harold's farm and help to comfort his mother. According to my sister, the lightning had melted the change in Harold's pockets and burned holes in his boots. It was a terrible experience for everyone, for my mother holding his mother tight as she looked on her dead son, for my dad, who had been standing right next to Harold when he was struck and who had helped carry him to his car, and, especially, for his own mother. Losing a child is the worst experience that any parent can undergo. My mother and father had already lost one son

Lawrence and I share a moment of rest at the front of the house while a rose bush spreads its blooms above our heads.

by then, their first born, Bernard, who had died in infancy. Although the rest of us children obviously never knew him, we all called him Bernie. Once a member of our family, always a member.

So my mother, perhaps remembering Harold's death, would rush all of us to the basement when a storm grew particularly violent. There we waited in damp, near-darkness for the storm to ease. My mother would bring a candle down with her. It gave a little light as we huddled among the shelves of canned tomatoes, strawberries, and peaches, a few of the older jars turning white. The main reason for the candle, though, was protection, not visibility. It was a sacred candle, one blessed by the priest, and my mother had an unshakeable confidence in its ability to preserve us from harm.

My mother liked to tell about the time that a storm came up fast, and in the turmoil and haste to reach the cellar everyone seemed to forget about the baby. I was the baby. My brother Lawrence raced up the steps, retrieved me, and hurried back down, the family complete. Although I did not know what was happening at the time, I appreciate the gesture, even if the house did survive the storm just fine and I surely would have been equally fine upstairs despite the tempest swirling about me. It is often, as in this case, the thought that counts.

Actually, my mother had a three-pronged approach to saving us from storms. One was the cellar itself, just in case all else failed; the second was the blessed candle; and the third was palm leaves, the kind that grows in warm climates, the kind that believers spread before Jesus on his way into Jerusalem.

Like other Catholics, we received palm on Palm Sunday leading up to Easter. My mother would drape the palm over pictures hanging on the wall, where it would be ready for an emergency. When a storm came up, she would burn a little of it in an ashtray. This burnt offering, actually a ritual with a long and broad historical context stretching back to Old Testament times and practiced by American Indians, though in different ways and for a variety of purposes, was something my mother strongly believed in. Her faith was deep, and it tended to be really concrete. Prayer was good, but something physical, like lighting a candle or burning some palm, made prayer work a lot better.

Of course, I do not know whether the candle or the burnt palm saved the day, but our house survived many ferocious storms when I was a child. But not so one of our barns.

As with several of the most traumatic events that befell my family,

Edward J. Rielly

including the death of Harold Flood, losing the barn to a tornado occurred before I was born. Making one's first appearance after a lot of significant family events have occurred is to be expected when one is the youngest of five children.

The barn was, strictly speaking, a hay barn as opposed to a cow barn. It is always better to lose crops than cattle, and so this loss was more easily overcome, emotionally and financially, than if our cows had been inside when the barn went down. The barn was rebuilt and served me well during my growing-up years as my special, and often only, baseball companion, a matter I give considerable attention to elsewhere in these pages.

Tornadoes seemed to be a special problem in our family. One also took the house where Grandfather and Grandmother McKeon, my mother's parents, had lived, and where Grandpa McKeon, then a widower, still lived. Luckily, he was not home when the tornado hit. Little was ever found, as the tornado basically reduced the house to splinters and deposited them across the countryside. Remnants of their old piano, though, were discovered along a nearby creek, a sad reminder of what had been lost.

My father once took me to Monroe, Wisconsin, to see the aftermath of a tornado that had ripped through the outskirts of the town. It happened in the spring, around Easter time. The devastation was great, and the scene of lost homes and overturned cars certainly hit home, especially for my father.

I now live where there are no tornadoes and where a serious lightning storm is a rarity. I do not miss them.

June Bugs

I generally have been able to take insects or leave them: no serious run-ins with poisonous spiders, no damaging bee bites, though an occasional insect sting induced a little redness and soreness from time to time. Flies always were a problem on the farm, but one we learned to live with. Oh, we killed the flies we could in the house but over all had a fatalistic approach to them. If you live on a farm, you will have flies. No two ways about that.

But June bugs were different, and I actually looked forward to their arrival. I liked their green and gold bodies, their ugly, horned heads that promised ferocity but gave only a gentle tickling to hands that cupped them. And it was easy to catch those bugs, especially at night.

With no air conditioning, we often sat in the kitchen with both the north and south doors open to allow a through breeze. Of course, we had screen doors, so not many June bugs made it into the kitchen. But I would listen to the small thuds as their small bodies, drawn by the kitchen light, hit the screen door. When an occasional June bug found a welcoming hole in the screen and trespassed on human territory, I would catch it (easy enough to do, as they were anything but agile), listen to the buzzing within my cupped hands, feel the tickling as the June bug sought its escape, and then step outside, open my hands in the yard, and let it fly away.

They also liked to buzz around the tall pole light that loomed just outside our back yard, casting a welcoming glow for visitors—the human and the insect kinds. The June bugs would swoop and careen through the lighted night, disappear into darkness, and reenter the yellow glare surrounding the tall pole. A stroll over to the pole light would almost guarantee a nearby buzz and a thud on my head or atop a shoulder as a June bug landed. They never did me any harm, though. I would just brush them off, and we would all go our separate ways.

To a casual observer, June bugs look like bumblebees. They are about the same size and share some of the same coloration. They also buzz, and they look even more dangerous. However, their gentle nature, their seeming desire to join our human community, made them a much happier emblem of warm summer nights on the farm than other insects. I kind of miss them at my door these days.

Edward J. Rielly

Growing Those Vegetables

We combined unhealthy food (lots of fried food, heavily laden with grease) with the "good stuff": fruits and vegetables. The vegetables were, for me, more fun to grow than eat, although there were exceptions. I loved onions and radishes.

Onions were my favorites, in their scallion stage before growing large bulbs, when most of what was there was green. I ate just about the whole onion, except the whiskers at the bottom. The white bottom I enjoyed, really just a small knob at most, but the greens were the best part, more for their performance than taste. Of course, they had to be prepared properly, which meant cutting the ends to transform the greens into straws. Then it was important to water them well by alternately slurping water upward and blowing into the water to raise nice big bubbles in the glass. The eating was anticlimactic.

Radishes were great rolled in salt. Peas and beans I ate only under strict orders from my mother. I needed no directions to consume potatoes and sweet corn. Both came to my plate from pots of boiling water, and both benefited from heavy coatings of butter and salt. Boiled potatoes are an Irish favorite, and my mother served them regularly at supper. The leftover potatoes she fried the following day for dinner, slicing the pieces thin and cooking them until they were crispy on the outside. I enjoyed sliced tomatoes with a dose of sugar or mayonnaise on each slice.

An army with fixed bayonets could not get me to consume beets, and I considered lettuce something best left to rabbits.

So given my mixed reaction to vegetables, why did I enjoy gardening so much?

As with many elements of my youth, I have no definitive explanation. It surely was not the weeding, which could get old pretty fast. Mainly, I think it was the planning, which led to a lot of daydreaming over seed catalogs. Catalogs came in winter when snow buried any trace of last year's garden.

I would open the seed catalog on the kitchen table in the evening and move methodically through it, page by page. The pictures were always grand. The vegetables evinced not a hint of disease or insect encroachment. The tomatoes were unalloyed red, each ear of sweet corn missed nary a kernel, and even the vegetables I detested, such as beets, looked almost enticing.

As I turned the pages, I marked the vegetables that I would like to plant. I was, naturally, wildly unrealistic. To plant everything I marked would have required my father to abandon every crop we depended on for a livelihood and plant the whole farm in vegetables—heresy for a dairy farmer. Secondly, we never actually ordered from the catalog. The catalog was for dreaming. Reality was a store in Darlington.

If I was not able to order tons of seeds from the catalog, I could at least accompany my mother to that feed store on a corner of Main Street to purchase seeds, and that was an adventure in itself. In fact, doing that was almost as much fun as journeying through the catalog.

A row of barrels stood in front of a long counter, and additional barrels were scattered throughout the store—each barrel full of seeds and a scoop. We would scoop out what we wanted into a brown paper bag. We scooped peas and beans (green and yellow), radish and lettuce seeds, the detested beet seeds, seeds for cucumbers and pumpkins, sweet corn, sometimes muskmelon seeds (which we never called cantaloupes), and, my favorite, small onion bulbs. We even tried raising watermelons occasionally but never had much luck with them—the growing season, I guess, being too short. Scooping out those seeds was as much fun as selecting candy from the glass cases in the Fair Store just up the street. Of course, we did not start with seeds for all of the vegetables, in some cases purchasing plants instead: tomato plants, cabbage plants, pepper plants.

Planting was prepared for by my father or one of my older brothers, who plowed the ground, then disked and harrowed it to make the soil smooth and soft. Yet despite that preparation, planting took a lot of effort. Different vegetables required different approaches, of course, but nothing was as laborious as planting the onion bulbs. With the edge of a hoe, I would make a trench. Then the bulbs had to go in right side up and be covered so that the small shoot just rising from the bulb would be protruding from the soil. If the bulb had not yet started to sprout, it would be completely covered, but not too deeply. A lot of work, but I was willing to do it to have my onions.

The tomato plants had to be hilled up carefully with dirt piled around them. We planted everything close enough not to waste space but not so close as to impede strong growth. And, of course, we planted in straight rows, running string down the length of the garden from one stake to another to ensure that the rows were straight and just the right distance apart. For a while, the garden could be cultivated with a tractor to remove a lot of the weeds and keep the soil soft and conducive for rain to work its magic. But after things had started growing and spreading, all of the weeding had to be done with a hoe or literally by hand, yanking the weeds out.

We watched our vegetable offspring carefully, anticipating their maturation. By the time the first vegetables were ready for the table, we were filled with excitement. Onions always came early. Sometimes the best is first.

Although my gustatory response to the vegetables was mixed, and I sometimes tired badly of the weeding, planning the garden was always a wonderful, imaginative escapade, and bringing the seeds home an adventure to remember. Now that I think of it, maybe those trees and bushes in my current backyard should go. Just think of all the onions I could grow.

The Old Shed

We had two sheds on our farm and drew sharp distinctions between them, both in naming and use. The large, relatively new building where we kept car, truck, and assorted farm equipment such as the hay bailer was the "machine shed." The much smaller and much older, as well as considerably more decrepit, building was the "old shed."

We stayed with basics in our naming. The old shed was the old shed because it was old. For years it seemed constantly on the verge of falling down in a good windstorm. Had we been so inclined, we could as well have called it the leaning shed. Almost everything about it leaned: its walls, the large doors that would no longer shut, the workbench at the back against the north wall, the roof that slanted in from both north and south.

But oh, how much fun it was to enter that shed. We primarily kept stuff there we no longer used, in truth, would likely never use again. An old oats binder spent its retirement in the old shed, steel wheels slowly rutting into the hard ground floor. Dust covered everything, generally tinged with a fine layer of grease. A heavier film of grease covered all the old tools, bolts, and nails on the workbench. Searching through the debris on the bench, for a child, was like digging for hidden treasure. Despite the grease that attached itself to my hands and crept under my fingernails, I kept digging. One never knew what might surface.

One day I came across an old pistol. No danger, as it lay there minus a crucial portion of its anatomy, its trigger. I have no idea where the pistol came from. I am sure that my father never owned one, but it might have gone back to his father. In my imagination, though, I saw it in the hand of a Civil War soldier, undoubtedly from Wisconsin, facing General Lee's troops. Or perhaps wielded by a cowboy who had made the long trek from the West to settle in this Midwestern farmland. Or maybe it just gravitated to the bench as a welcome spot to sink into eternity surrounded by other old, grease-covered metal objects.

If there are two things you can be sure of on a farm, they are (1) that objects accumulate, and (2) that nothing gets thrown away. Everything gets set someplace. The workbench was one of those places designated for setting objects no longer in use. There is always the concern that someday a need might arise for that bolt, screw, rusted hinge, piece of wire, or broken ax handle. Hence, nothing gets thrown away; things just keep accumulating. These habits result in countless hours of delight for farm children. The most obscure objects may become childhood treasures.

I remember when the machine shed was brand new. I might even say that the interior was neat—everything stacked, sorted, stored—for a time. Of course, objects started accumulating there, too. But the objects

Edward J. Rielly

tended to be newer, less coated with grease, quoting better odds for being used again. The workbench had to be kept reasonably clear so it could actually be used for such practices as measuring, sawing, drilling, and the like. I admired the machine shed, but I loved the old shed. It was a matter of distinctions.

Home Delivery

One of the realities of my life growing up on our farm was that we were a good distance from town. We were not isolated completely, but at the same time going to town was not something we could manage every day. My parents were busy people, and my mother did not drive. There is a story to my mother not driving, but that story I address elsewhere.

So home delivery was of some importance. Catalog buying had developed with farm families in mind. Back in 1872, a traveling salesman named Aaron Montgomery Ward issued a single-sheet listing of 163 mail-order objects. By 1875, Ward's "catalog" had expanded to seventy-two pages and included illustrations. When I was growing up, the Montgomery Ward (or as we sometimes fondly called it, "Monkey Ward") catalog was hundreds of pages long. Along with the Sears Roebuck catalog, and various seed catalogs, it provided lots of material for daydreaming and some for practical purchases.

One of the highlights of my day was the mail delivery. Looking forward to the mail started when I was very young and has never deserted me, despite my wife's queries about what wonderful communications I'm expecting. In fact, that rural mailman brought lots of goodies, albeit not on a daily basis, to our farm. Some of the items were from catalogs. Others were books.

Early on I developed a great passion for reading. With no bookstores in my hometown and many miles between the nearest one and me, I joined the Book of the Month Club. Fortunately, we had a large mailbox (situated on top of an old milk can painted white), and there was plenty of room inside for a good-sized book. My library began to grow, each mail delivery of my reading matter covering another inch or two of shelf space. Then one shelf led to another, until today whole rooms in my house are filled with books, books spreading like the Blob from that old science-fiction movie. But no purchasing of books today in a huge bookstore can equal the anticipation and joy involved in seeing the mailman stick a box from the Book of the Month Club into our mailbox.

Some might consider sliding from books to pigs to be a rapid descent from the sublime to the ridiculous, but not so. We bought a variety of things that came by delivery to our farm. One of them was a white pig that my father purchased for me from a truck driver traveling about the countryside selling young pigs from his truck. I believe that it was a Chester White. My father bought a white pig for me so that it would not get mixed up with all the other, dark-colored pigs. We raised it to adulthood and then sold it. I received the money. Those books were expensive.

The ice cream truck also came to our farm, not the little vehicle with bells ringing and music blaring that people encounter on city streets today. This was a good-sized truck, its cab perhaps the size of a pickup's but with a large metallic box behind that served as a freezer on wheels. The driver sold ice cream products and meat. We were not big customers, but sometimes we bought ice cream. One of the problems with living twelve miles from town, and usually driving those twelve miles at about forty miles per hour over dusty gravel roads, is that on a hot, humid summery day things like ice cream tend to degenerate from solids to liquids by the time you get home. So the home-delivery ice cream truck had its place.

So much else came our way out on the farm. The tall cylinders of gas for our gas stove were delivered by truck. Salesmen came by selling a variety of merchandise and services. We could sit in the kitchen and buy a new vacuum cleaner or lean against the pickup out beside the barn and contract to have that barn newly whitewashed. But no deliveryman or salesman ever excited me the way that the mailman did, especially when I was anticipating the arrival of a book.

Edward J. Rielly

Fencing: the Barbed Wire Type, Not the Sport

Dairy farming encompasses a multitude of jobs that never end, starting, of course, with milking, which occurs twice each day forever. There are no days off. But other jobs also continue, repeated ad infinitum if not ad nauseam, from feeding cows, pigs, sheep, chickens, and any other creatures that roam the farm, to cleaning the barn of cowish deposits that equally never cease. Then, just as unabatedly, are the farm wife's chores, including the meals (three a day) and a variety of other inside and outside tasks, in my mother's case, washing clothes, hanging them out to dry on our clothesline, feeding chickens, gardening, and many other tasks.

Fencing is not as regular as these functions, not as clockwork regulated, but if one does not have to focus every day on building and rebuilding fences, it is still a job that never journeys too far from a farmer's consciousness.

The main culprits behind weakened fences are cows. Cows are heavy animals, and they have a disturbing tendency to lean toward what they want. Barbed wire may impede, but it also has a fair amount of give in it when a heavy beast pushes. And if a section of wire gives way, those cows may soon be in the middle of a cornfield doing substantial harm to the crop and themselves. Overeating is not healthy for man or cow.

In addition to fences around fields of crops, there are the fences around pastures. On the other side often lies, or curves, a gravel road that leads to other places owned by other farmers, who are not real keen on having any strange cows moving in on their territory. Motorists also tend to resent a heavy cow positioning itself in the middle of the road. A dented hood might well be the least of that driver's problems.

The serious consequences of a gap in a fence mean that fencing does indeed remain a constant. So my father did a lot of fencing, by that time mostly repair work as everything that needed to be fenced already was enclosed. My older brothers also worked at this before leaving the farm, one to move to Rockford, Illinois, another to take over his own farm. I often, as the saying goes, lent a hand.

A clever man named Joseph Glidden invented barbed wire in 1873. That led to many disputes between farmers and ranchers in the Old West, but it was a lifesaver to Wisconsin farmers when I was growing up—and perhaps literally a lifesaver to more than one motorist passing by. Barbed wire can solve many problems and is probably as major an invention as Saltine crackers or sliced bread. If something, almost anything, was falling apart, my dad seemed able to wire it together.

The wire came on spools for reasonably easy unraveling. The basic tools included a wire cutter and heavy gloves to protect fingers from the barbs. A pair of pliers came in handy for twisting wire, and wire fasteners went around the metal posts to hold the wire in place. Of course, if we were attaching wire to the heavy wooden corner posts, we needed a hammer and staples.

Many times all we needed to do was cut a piece of barbed wire and use it to splice two broken pieces of wire. Barbed wire twists nicely, and quickly that gap would be filled. Of course, if we were attaching a lengthy strip of wire, perhaps replacing wire between a few posts, a wire stretcher would come in handy to make the wire taut and less likely to yield to a cow's pushing.

The heaviest part of fencing involved replacing metal posts that had become bent. Here a sledgehammer came into play. I learned to swing one pretty well, quickly improving my aim. A misguided swing could, at best, hit only air rather than the post and cause some momentary embarrassment; at worst, it might endanger the hand holding the post steady. One can easily see that driving posts required two people for efficiency: one to hold until the post reached far enough into the ground to sit steadily, and one to swing.

It's funny how certain images remain with you. I can still see my father twisting barbed wire. Always his hands. Not how he looked at the wire, not how he swung the sledgehammer, but just his hands as he twisted the wire. I cannot think of barbed wire in particular—or of fencing in general—without seeing him and his hands. When I drive in posts around a flower garden these days, he could almost be there beside me.

Edward J. Rielly

Mr. Wade the Pump Man

East of our house, just beyond our lawn fence and the gate that led toward the gravel driveway and our barns, was a cement platform. A hydrant rose from the platform, and a circular covering, much like a manhole cover, hid the entrance to a small square room underground. There, in that dark, dank interior were the workings of our pump system that made drew water from the deep recesses of the earth and distributed it to the hydrant above, a hydrant near the barnyard, and the faucets within our house.

This system worked well except when it did not. And when that happened, my dad summoned Mr. Wade the pump man to make things right again.

The periodic arrival of Mr. Wade (whose first name I never knew, although presumably my parents did) was always entertaining. He was— and remains—probably the thinnest man I have ever seen. This would have been cause enough for some humorous entertainment were it not also for the inexplicable fact that Mr. Wade, the very thin man, could wield tools—especially large, bulky wrenches—that seemed to weigh almost as much as he did. I half expected him to topple over as he carried his tools from his truck to the pump room, but his spindly arms gave no quarter to the weight of their load.

But I get ahead of myself. First, there was his truck. He always drove the same truck, whose make and model I am as ignorant of as his first name. However, it was black and very old. It likely appeared from its primitive assembly line sometime in the 1930s. A flapping fender and a crack that slithered down one of the door windows punctuated its antiquity. It was not, though, as old as Mr. Wade, who combined considerable age with thinness and an antique truck to make my day whenever he appeared.

I never really talked with him, except to say hello, but I would stand and watch him disappear into the cement pump room with his oversized wrenches, stretching my neck as far as possible to peer down through the opening and attempt to follow what he was doing. What-ever it was, it worked. Always. Mr. Wade, despite his lack of youth and weight, could fix our pumping system, which he did with great skill many times.

Then Mr. Wade would place his tools back into the box of his an-tique truck and depart. And once again the water would flow to our cows and to our house until the next time that we needed a very thin man in a very old black truck.

The Old Silo

A farm is filled with sensory perceptions. All of the five senses (sight, smell, taste, hearing, and touch for those who do not recall what they are) come into play. The silo was right up there, regarding stimulat-ing the senses, with the barn and kitchen. As a matter of fact, it was up there in height as well. To a boy, the silo seemed even taller than it was, especially when I had to climb it.

First, the purpose of the silo: it was built to hold silage, which is chopped corn (the whole shebang: ears, stalks, and leaves). Silage was cattle food for the winter when there was no grass and the cows had to be kept indoors except for a brief excursion into the barnyard for a drink.

The cows had a diet of hay, ground oats, and silage in the winter, a pretty good diet as cow diets go. The hay came from hay bales stored upstairs in the barn, so the bales had to be tossed down the two hay chutes. Ground oats waited in sacks brought from the feed mill. We hauled oats into town and returned with the sacks of ground feed. Silage had to be tossed down from the silo into the silage room, which opened into the barn.

The silo was ringed on the outside with metal rings, but no one crawled up the outside, although the silo was open at the top. Inside the silage room, which connected the silo to the barn, there was a wooden chute running up one side of the silo. A metal ladder was affixed per-

Edward J. Rielly

manently to the exterior of the silo, inside the chute, with one footrest directly below each of the wooden doors that opened into the silo. So I would crawl up the ladder, protected by the wooden chute from the wind, my foot placed carefully on metal steps that often were coated with ice and therefore slippery. I would open the topmost door and crawl through onto the silage. A wide-tined fork was my implement for forking silage through the door and down the chute into the silage room.

At first, the silo would be just about full of silage. The top of the silage could get really frozen in bad weather, as snow, of course, dropped right onto it. As winter progressed, the level of silage dropped steadily, and I would not have to climb as high. I also chipped any frozen silage off the sides so that we did not leave a layer of silage lining the inside of the silo, which not only would be a waste but also would mold and therefore be useless as feed.

Returning to ground, I would step into a large pile of silage I had just forked down. The silage went into a large metal basket, which I carted down the rows of stanchions, dropping some in front of each of the cows, their anxious heads often getting in the way as they batted the bucket in their haste to eat. They loved that stuff.

So about the senses: silage has a sweet (kind of sickly sweet) odor that is not especially pleasant to a human. The smell often would accompany my dad and me into the house after we finished the milking and related chores. Touch was a big part of the process, my gloved hands holding on tight to the metal bars as I climbed, the feel of silage, frozen on the top but soft as I got down a bit into it. Or the soft, wet tongues of cows licking my hands as I poured the silage. Even from high in the silo, I could hear the silage plopping onto the cement floor at the base of the chute. The metal basket rattled almost rhythmically as cows, one after another, bunted it, impatiently reaching for their meal. Fortunately, I did not have to taste the silage, but the cows sure did, much to their pleasure. Sight: well, I guess that I already have covered that in my description. So the senses came into play really well in and around the silo, so much so that I can still smell that silage and feel the cold, slippery ladder that I climbed so high, with the stars lighting my way on cold winter evenings long ago

Waving

Every culture has its set of courtesies, acts that people naturally do to be polite, friendly, and neighborly. No law demands that a person follow the pattern, and no one will end up in jail for failing to live up to the set standards. One might come in for some criticism, probably not, though, to one's face. "Did you notice what so and so doesn't bother to do? Can you believe it?" That sort of thing.

Waving is one of these cultural actions deeply ingrained in rural life, at least back when I was growing up in Wisconsin. People waved. When we passed someone on a gravel road, we all waved. Often, especially close to home, we were likely to know each other, so waving would be socially required. Not to wave would be to come across as stuck up, and no one wanted to be labeled that way. We might not like the person driving the other vehicle, but that did not excuse us from the obligation to wave.

As we got farther from our farm, we still waved. If it did not matter whether we liked the person, it also did not matter whether we knew the person. We were expected to wave, and we did.

Most people, I have found, wave in largely similar ways, or at least in ways that do not stand out. The objective is to wave, not to make a production of it. Sometimes, however, a wave does prove distinctive. A neighbor of ours, Fred Hess, had a decidedly distinctive way of waving. I think of his wave as the windshield-wiper version. He did it with one finger. Lifting a single finger might be more than offensive to most people, depending on what one did with that finger. But Fred Hess did nothing offensive with his solitary finger. He raised that index finger and rotated it right and left, the way a windshield wiper moves. I do not recall ever seeing anyone else wave quite that way.

It would be nice if everyone were unique in some way. Mr. Hess was unique in his wave. I remember it well.

Edward J. Rielly

II.
The Big White Farmhouse

The Morris Chair

The most distinctive piece of furniture in our house was our Morris chair, named after its English popularizer, William Morris, a skilled craftsman who also was a poet of some renown. It was, I always felt, our throne, and since like most farm families we were bred to hospitality, our throne was especially there for our guests.

It sat in our kitchen, just inside the back door, the door we almost always used. The guest would enter and step to the right and be ready to occupy our seat of honor. Of course, it worked best if we had only one guest, because we had only one Morris chair.

The chair had a tall back and a firm, cushioned seat. As one sat in it, to the right was an armrest in the form of a long rectangular drawer with a hinged lid that came up. We kept assorted objects there, such as gloves or anything we needed a quick home for. The lid made a nice armrest. To the left was another armrest, with a slatted magazine rack built in below it.

That Morris chair now sits in a screen house behind our home in Maine, but it always looks a little out of place, as if it should be in our kitchen, waiting to embrace our latest visitor.

That Morris chair always takes me back to our farmhouse kitchen, and especially one visitor, a man named Nile, who lived a modest walk south of us in a house that used to be a cheese factory. Nile's father, Roscoe Evans, used to be a cheese maker, and before I was born my father and older brothers would haul milk there to be made into cheese. An older brother, Milton, lived with them, the other siblings having married and moved away.

Only Nile, though, came to visit. He would walk up perhaps twice a week and take his place in the Morris chair. He always politely resisted my mother's offers of food, though sometimes on a particularly hot day he would accept a cold drink.

Edward J. Rielly

Nile seemed old to me when I was very young, but he was one of those men who look old when young and then stay that way the rest of their life, seeming to have done all their aging in youth and then settling in for a good long run unchanged.

Nile really took to me and brought me pictures he had drawn. I no longer have it but vividly remember a large drawing of a road grader, an object we regularly saw grading our gravel roads in summer and plowing snow in winter. It was a detailed, thoroughly realistic, impeccably drawn road grader. In fact, Nile liked my whole family and seemed to adopt us as an extension of his own family.

We almost never missed seeing Nile's arrival, his climbing the incline into our front yard and slowly walking up through the yard. We had a good view out the front kitchen windows, and our front yard, being big, gave us plenty of time to notice him. "Here comes Nile," was a common saying. We appreciated the visits, although sometimes when my mother was especially busy there might have been a little mixture of emotion.

Nile had more time to visit than a lot of people, the result of one arm rendered almost useless by polio. When he was young, he did some chores around our farm, nothing too heavy, but things he could handle with one good arm. As a result of that bad arm, he was never able to drive a car. The good aspect of that disability for us was that he became a regular visitor, our being within easy walking distance.

Years later, after my father had died and we children had moved away, my mother still living, now alone, on the farm, Nile made a point of checking in on her regularly. It was the sort of thing good neighbors do. When we traveled back to Wisconsin to visit relatives, I usually stopped in to see Nile, only a little out of duty, until his recent death. He lived in town by himself in his last years, his father and Milton dead, and the old cheese factory sold. Our farm is sold, too. Much changes, but some things don't, like one's appreciation for a good neighbor.

Nile Again

Another memory I have of Nile is running into him, Milton, and their father in the grocery store. They would go shopping together, slowly pushing a grocery cart down the aisles, carefully choosing their foods. It was the kind of scene people are more likely to encounter, or at least notice, in a small town. And it is all the more memorable if you know the people. I once wrote a poem about their grocery shopping and place it here rather than try to describe the situation all over again in prose:

A Constant Pace

Pushing the cart down the aisle, wearing blue bib
overalls and high work shoes, the old man, now ninety-
six, moves slowly, keeping to the middle. He follows
his elder son, sixty-nine, who, without comment,
glances at a slip of paper, selects saltines, a can
of peaches, Cream of Wheat. Each item he places carefully

Joe, left, and Nile Evans shock oats in preparation for threshing.

Edward J. Rielly

in the cart. Even when the old man grumbles at the price
of coffee, he says nothing. The level in the cart rises
slowly. Then comes the youngest, still in his fifties,
who trails silently for a time, then waits at the counter.
Later he takes their two bags, places them side by side in
the trunk of their '72 Buick. All three squeezed in front,
the elder son driving, they pull out, inch down
the incline to the street. They drive home slowly,
following the dusty gravel road as it curves through
the woods, to the old cheese factory where they live,
the large silver vats empty in the basement. That night
the old man cooks dinner, cautiously measuring all things
at his pace. They pay no attention to the wind that rises
slowly, then moves through the trees, methodically
dropping a layer of dry leaves on the autumn grass.

I also wrote a poem just about Nile, and here it is:

The Man With One Good Arm

His one good arm did double
duty for the bad, the left
hanging straight down his side,
certainly not lifeless, twitching,
feeling, could move a bit,
sometimes even without help.
But for lifting and throwing
everything depended on the right.

And when he did chores around
our farm, a sometime hired hand
(in his case quite literally),
he hoisted with the right, carrying
pails that seemed heavy with indignity,
bested by a man with one good arm.

A hay bale was a consummate challenge
requiring careful placement of

his left hand on the baling twine,
fingers squeezing what they could,
the right swinging back and lifting,
his whole body heaved into the throw.
The effort took more careful planning,
more time to execute, a lot more

energy than he had most days. So
my dad would ease him into things
that required less, that could be done
without expecting much from one arm
that he had carried since childhood almost
as a thing apart, an alien appendage.

An old man now, he sits in his soft
chair and handles the television remote
easily, the sort of effort made
for one good arm. And when he dies
I imagine he will reach carefully with
his good right arm, hoist the left across
his belt and hug himself into eternity,
the two arms finally being equal.

Our First Freezer

Buying a freezer may not seem like a thrilling event to a lot of people,
but it surely was for me. Even today it's hard to define precisely why
I was so excited about the freezer.

It certainly was not much to look at—a big rectangular box with a
heavy lid that always threatened to come crashing down on whoever
was bent over, leaning in to fish out that hunk of meat or box of ice
cream.

There's no doubt that the freezer made life easier for my mother. Food, especially frozen meat, was at her fingertips whenever she wanted a pot roast, chicken, or some pork chops. Pull out a package, let it thaw, and stick it in the oven. That beat going to town to get two or three packages of meat at a time out of the locker where we stored our meat after butchering. We had no good way to keep much food frozen when I was a child, just a very small freezer compartment in the refrigerator, which was big enough to handle a little ice cream and a couple of ice-cube trays, but not much else. Yet, when we eventually got a freezer, I do not recall myself rejoicing because of some altruistic recognition that we were easing my mother's burden.

Yet I remember the discussions between my mother and father about buying that freezer and weighing in on the side of buying. My father was reluctant, given the cost. I have no idea today of the actual price, but given our modest finances, it clearly was a big investment for my parents.

Yes, the ice cream had something to do with it. I can still remember, over these many decades, my excitement when we were visiting neighbors one evening. The incident struck me so forcefully that I can still recall the film playing on their little black-and-white television: *The Fighting Sullivans*, the film about the five Sullivan brothers who served and died together on the same battleship during World War II. It was not the film, though, that excited me. It was the ice cream. And not the fact of ice cream, for I had enjoyed plenty of ice cream, but the size of the container: a whole gallon! A gallon of vanilla it was. I was so taken with the size of the container that I must not have noticed who dipped out the ice cream or I probably would remember that too. We had no way in our house of keeping a gallon of ice cream frozen, but George Jentz and family did—in their freezer. It was not long before we got our own freezer.

Maybe it was the ice cream that sealed the deal.

The Far Room

Our farmhouse was big, very big. So big that we used only about two-thirds of it for daily living purposes, and even that gave us a huge kitchen, dining room, parlor, two bathrooms (eventually), four bedrooms, and assorted closets plus a beautiful stairway to the second floor. The other one-third consisted of two mammoth rooms, one downstairs and one up. Both, of course, had doors between them and our living space, but they usually remained shut.

For a brief period of time after my brother Lawrence was married, he and his wife lived in those two rooms, but later the rooms went back to being what they were used for during almost all of the years I was growing up. The downstairs room had no special name. My mother washed clothes there, using her old wringer washing machine, then hanging the clothes out to dry on a pair of long clotheslines. If she needed more drying space, she just used the yard fence. We also stored stuff in the room, such as the lawnmower, generally things we tended to use at least occasionally.

The upper room, however, did have a name: the Far Room. The name made sense, I guess, in the farthest western portion of the house, even if, strictly speaking, it was just beyond the walls of two of our bedrooms.

There is a television show called *American Pickers*. The Pickers would have gone crazy in our Far Room. Everything that we no longer used but that my mother did not want to throw away, which was just about everything we ever owned, went into the Far Room. For a child, the room was irresistible, a kind of jungle with treasures under every tree.

There were old dressers, each drawer full, of course, each top covered in multi-layers of objects. Boxes and even an old wooden barrel invited delving for subterranean gems. Coats decades old hung from wooden racks like dead animals draped on limbs. Two windows allowed a pittance of light into the room, and one overhead bulb did not help a whole lot. The general darkness demanded a flashlight if one really

Edward J. Rielly

wanted to do any serious searching, and that is what I did far more times than I could possibly estimate today.

One of my discoveries remains especially vivid in my memory, perhaps because I was a serious reader then (as now) and had a special love for history. The magazine was *Life*, and the article was about the exhumation of Abraham Lincoln in 1901 when the president's tomb was being reconstructed. The casket was opened to make sure that Lincoln was still there, a concern real enough given a previous effort to steal the body. There were photographs of the exhumation but not of Lincoln himself, although the body's condition was described in vivid detail. The story was one that would appeal to the imagination of a lot of children, children tending toward the gruesome on occasion.

When my mother died, years after my father passed away, we spent hours clearing out the Far Room. My sister, Mary; brother, Joe; and I arranged for a dumpster (a very big dumpster) to be parked outside below a window, and we tossed most of the room's contents out. Of course, we salvaged some things, but most went out the window. It was a shame. Seems as if something a person saves should be saved, but that's not the way it works. Clearing out the room was both physically and emotionally tasking. So much of all of us was still piled there, but we had no real choice. Maybe if the Pickers had come along years earlier, they would have helped to deplete the pile while giving a new life to portions of it.

With the dumpster parked outside the window, we started going through the material, helped by my son and brother-in-law. My sister and I passed judgment on which items should be saved, a difficult evaluation indeed. Everything else we tossed out the window. The dumpster was, I think, the largest size one could rent, and before we finished it was full to overflowing. I walked around it, taking a final look at the contents, those that were poking out. A lot called out to me, but I resisted, except for a cowboy hat, white with black cowboys circling it, and with my childhood name, "Eddie," written on the brim. I also grabbed an old lunchbox, but everything else I let go.

A few years after we sold the farm, I visited the new owners. They were very nice and invited me in to see the changes that they had made. What a mistake, my accepting the invitation! The stairway had been closed off, with other alterations in the downstairs. But what really got me was the Far Room. It was now a bedroom, their master bedroom, with lights and everything. How could they do that? There should have been boxes full of items—new boxes perhaps, but still, boxes—and a general jumble working its way back toward the clutter that I remember fondly. Change can be very difficult. I will never visit the farmhouse again. Seriously.

Honeybees in the Chimney

I just spent some time talking about the "Far Room" in our farmhouse. Without repeating what I said, I want to recount an incident which once upon a time affected that room: an infestation of honeybees.

The Far Room included a chimney, but during most of my growing-up years the room was not inhabited, instead serving as a catch-all storage area. The chimney thus remained unused as there was no need to keep the Far Room and the room directly underneath it heated.

Somehow a swarm of honeybees caught wind of the unused chimney and decided that it offered a comfortable and safe haven for their abode. So they settled in and started doing what honeybees do: making honey.

Now I very much liked honey—and still do—but both I and the rest of my family were satisfied with an occasional jar of honey from the grocery store. In my case, a purchased square of honeycomb was a special treat, and I would eat that comb by the spoonful.

Actually raising honeybees, however, was hardly necessary given the modest amount of honey that we consumed. In addition, my father and older brothers had plenty to do with our more standard farm crops—hay, oats, corn—and the great amount of work involved in running a dairy farm. No one had any appetite (a pun I cannot resist) for harvesting honey.

And although no one actually lived in the Far Room, we did not appreciate the presence of honeybees when we did enter the room to search for something stored away there. So what to do about the honeybees?

Edward J. Rielly

It so happened that a neighbor of ours to the north raised bees as a sideline. Might he be interested in gathering another swarm for an additional beehive? Yes, he was.

So Mr. Coulthard came for the bees. And he came prepared: a protective hat and net that hung down over his face, thick gloves, and sturdy clothing to prevent bee stings elsewhere on his body. He had a large net as I recall. Of course, I kept my distance, so I cannot testify to each technique that he employed to entice the bees out of our chimney and into a suitable container for transporting. However, he succeeded in ridding our chimney of the honeybees.

Once again we could explore the Far Room for whatever treasure we wanted to unearth, albeit with a warm sweater or coat on during winter months, without fear of an attack by freeloading honeybees seeking to call our home theirs.

Flies

I mention flies in my entry on June bugs but do not get deeply into the subject. I mention that we killed what flies we could in the house but fail to offer our strategies. Since flies were omnipresent on our farm but decidedly not welcome in our house, and ridding the house of flies, an ultimately eternal and impossible task, was a major concern of my mother, passing too lightly over the subject, I am afraid, would leave an improper gap.

So back to the flies.

We tolerated them outside, partly because flies on a farm are a part of the nature of things, and also because we could do virtually nothing about them. We were as helpless to prevent flies in the barn or barnyard as were the cows that faced endless buzzing about their faces. I felt sorry for the cows because I could at least shoo flies away from my face, one of the advantages of having hands, something cows are sorely lacking.

In the house, however, we waged constant warfare with flies. I hesitate even to think of the cans containing horrible chemicals that we sprayed to kill them. Yes, we used DDT before it was outlawed. Those were the innocent days when, if someone sold an item in a store, you assumed that it was okay.

Most of the time, though, we resorted to two other weapons: the fly swatter and flypaper. There are certain keys to using fly swatters effectively. First, one must have several of them strategically placed throughout the house. If one has to go to another room to get a fly swatter, the fly has almost certainly skedaddled before the would-be fly slaughterer can return. Second, even having a fly swatter in each room is insufficient. Let's say that you are sitting in your easy chair watching *I Love Lucy* on television and an annoying fly keeps buzzing about your head. The fly swatter, though in the room, is actually deposited on top of the television. You see the problem, don't you? By the time that you return to your chair with the fly swatter, that fly also has disappeared. A fly will hang around for what seems like hours, but the moment you move it heads out for a new victim to torture. Flies are not stupid.

So the key is to have a fly swatter close at hand. It should be within easy reach of your right hand (left hand if you are left-handed) so that you can pick up the fly swatter without moving any portion of your body except for the hand. Then you must be able to raise the swatter without moving your head, thus tricking the fly into thinking that you are doing nothing more harmful than perhaps scratching behind an ear. Then WHAM!!!

We learned to be tremendously accurate with a fly swatter—no easy accomplishment. Mickey Mantle hitting a curve ball had an easier time. But I learned to anticipate the fly's possible move and catch the fly under the meaty part of the swatter just as it was lifting off. I had to clean my fly swatter many times.

Now that you know how to master the fly swatter, I will turn to another primary weapon, one that required no skill whatsoever. All one had to do with flypaper was hang it from the ceiling with the attached tack and pull one end toward the floor so that the paper stretched downward in its long, narrow strip. Flypaper is really sticky, so any fly that lands on it stays put. After a while, the fly dies. After a greater while, the flypaper is covered with deceased flies.

Edward J. Rielly

No skill required at all. However, a long strip of sticky paper covered in dead flies is not an especially appealing sight. I do not recommend hanging one over the kitchen table. Using a fly swatter is much neater, assuming that one cleans up consistently. It also is a wonderful instrument for developing hand-eye coordination. I often wonder why baseball coaches do not routinely hand out fly swatters with bats, balls, gloves, and uniforms.

Porches

Our house had two porches that we used, one facing south toward our large front yard and the row of pine trees bordering the gravel road that passed by our home. The other was a smaller back porch north of the house. Both were off our kitchen.

We used the back porch a lot more often as it led directly to the barn and other buildings by way of a cement sidewalk that headed due east toward a small metal gate and, beyond the gate, our underground pump room, the gravel driveway, and then our barns. Most people visiting also arrived by way of the back porch.

The porch was made of cement and was painted red. It had a wooden roof and housed an old kitchen cook stove that had taken up residency against the kitchen wall, consigned to holding occasional materials of transitory importance. It also served as a workbench on which we could deposit whatever we wished. I suspect that it remained on the porch primarily because it was too heavy to move any farther.

I recall filling in cracks and holes when the porch was recemented. At that time, I implanted my handprint in the wet cement, where it hardened and may still reside. We always referred to it as the "cement porch," not the back porch, probably because, although technically it was our back porch, it actually received far more traffic than the front porch.

The front porch, however, was the "front porch." We never referred to it as the wooden porch. I am sure that we never thought out these names; they just happened.

The front porch included stately wooden columns, giving the house a regal, almost Southern look. We had a couple of metal chairs on the porch but did not often use them. Farmers do not have a lot of time for sitting on porches.

At some point, a swing had hung from the porch roof. I have no memory of it, but the large hooks that once held it remained, firmly fixed in the roof.

Many lightning storms would arrive from a southerly direction, and, while they remained at a distance, we might step out onto the front porch to watch the distant fireworks. When the storm got close, though, we sought the safety of indoors—and, as I indicate elsewhere, the cellar if the storm grew especially violent.

So the front porch was primarily there for, one might say, aesthetic reasons, for it added to the beauty of the house. The cement porch was the workaday porch. And then there was another wooden porch, similar to the one just described, also looking southward but stretching out from the western portion of our house, from the large room directly below the "Far Room." We did not use that porch. It just sat there, offering an attractive symmetry to the front of our house.

Doors and Locks

Like most farm families in our neighborhood, we did not think much about keeping our house locked. One unstated reason that I believe played a role in our modest concern for home security was that none of the other buildings—the barns, machine shed, pig houses, etc.—had locks on them, and a thief was apt to find plenty of value in them, including, of course, valuable animals. The house probably offered less enticing assets. The primary reason, however, was that we trusted our neighbors and did not anticipate strangers happening along with larceny in their hearts.

Edward J. Rielly

Our most often used doors opened into our kitchen. They were wooden and accompanied by screen doors that we regularly used in summer—in the absence of air conditioning, a luxury neither we nor our neighbors even contemplated having back in those days—to introduce a cooling breeze into the kitchen. We therefore often kept the wooden doors open.

The screen doors, which kept out insects, some of them at least, could be locked by way of a hook that went into an eye screwed into the wooden framework. The hook would keep no one out who wanted to enter, a slight pull easily sending the hook clattering to the floor, but that hook at least worked against a sudden gust of wind blowing the door open and admitting a rush of insects, especially at night when the kitchen lights attracted them.

As a child, I do not remember our ever locking the north door, the one leading onto the cement porch. For some reason, we occasionally locked the southern door, which we accomplished by sliding a small bolt into its holder from the inside. Perhaps we simply did not have a key with which to lock the northern door. In truth, the practice makes little sense to me now, as visitors seldom entered the house through the southern door, and if some stranger might actually have hiked up through the front yard and tried yanking open the door, he would, one surmises, have simply walked around the house to the opposite door, which he would have found yielding easily to a slight turn of the doorknob. Fortunately, we never had any trouble with anyone breaking into our house. We never, so far as I can recall, worried about it. It was a time when people, at least in rural southwestern Wisconsin, did not have to worry about locking their doors.

The Parlor

If our house conveyed a sort of southern mansion look with the colonnaded front porch, it also boasted that type of genteel room known as a parlor. For some reason, they usually are referred to as front parlors, perhaps because they typically are located in the front portion of the house. That was the case with our parlor. Its large window looked out onto our front lawn. Well, it would have done so had the view not been largely obstructed by bushes, especially a huge mock orange bush, and a fine, upstanding pine tree that indeed stood very up. We just let it keep growing, and it paid us back for our tolerance by providing shade. The parlor usually was the coolest room in the house, partly because of the shade but also because, with the only window facing south, it did not get much direct sunlight.

So we did not see a lot through the window, although just enough sunlight entered to keep alive the large array of house plants resting on a multi-layered plant stand inside the window. Many of those plants were mine, as I early on developed an interest in plants that has grown, my wife might say, entirely out of control in recent years.

So we had a parlor. It was a comfortable room with a davenport, a couple of large, soft chairs, and other furniture, such as a bookcase in which I arranged my growing, yet by today's standards, still rather small collection of books, including those books I received from the Book of the Month Club. By the way, my gathering of books has exceeded even my collecting of plants.

Yet despite the comfort, quiet, and all around pleasantness of the parlor, we did not use it much—perhaps for the same reason we did not much use the front porch. Farmers do not have a lot of time for sitting. In addition, although parlors usually are associated with entertaining visitors, our visitors usually were dropping in for just a couple of hours, so we tended to stay in the kitchen, close to the coffee pot.

However, when I wanted some solitude for reading, the parlor worked really well. It was one of my reading places, along with my bedroom and a very tall maple tree in the far corner of our orchard (more about that later).

The parlor occasionally also served other purposes. When I developed a temporary heart condition in grade school, leakage in a heart valve associated with rheumatic fever, the parlor served as my temporary bedroom. Many years later, when Dad's health declined, it served a similar purpose for him. Regrettably, we do not have a parlor in our

Edward J. Rielly

current house. More urbanized now, I would have enough time to put it to good visiting use, along, of course, with spending some quality reading time in it.

Stovepipes

If someone might guess affluence from our front porches and the existence of a parlor, a quick reference to stovepipes should rectify that misconception. The reality was that our house was cold in winter. We had two stoves: one in the kitchen and one in the dining room (between the kitchen and parlor) to provide heat. Later, we put in a furnace, which changed the ambient temperature dramatically, but during my childhood we had only two stoves, both located on the ground floor. However, we all slept on the second floor, minus stoves, fireplaces, or heaters of any sort.

What we relied on upstairs were vents in the floor and stovepipes. Neither did all that much, but they helped a bit. The best antidote to being cold, of course, was to change into pajamas as fast as possible and jump into bed, pulling covers layer by layer up to one's chin.

However, for those who had a stovepipe climbing through their rooms—just two rooms, although one was my bedroom during my adolescence—the stovepipe offered a bonus. Here's the trick: While fully clothed, place your pajamas on the floor around the stovepipe, wait until they are as hot as possible (ideally just before they burst into flames), and then change into the pajamas as rapidly as you can.

Now, you probably do not have stovepipes in your house today, but just in case you end up in a house with stoves and stovepipes, do not claim that I failed to offer you some practical advice on how to maintain a level of comfort at least bordering on warmth.

Down in the Cellar

The cellar, as I noted earlier, was the final refuge during fierce storms. It also served other purposes, especially relating to food. The cellar had an earth floor and cement walls. The combination kept the cellar cool and damp in summer and relatively warm (at least not freezing) in winter. Thus it was the repository for the Mason jars of food that my mother canned. She primarily canned fruits and vegetables: apples and cherries from our orchard; beans, tomatoes, pickles, and other vegetables from our garden. Sometimes she canned other foods as well, such as gooseberries, strawberries, and even beef.

Shelves rose from the floor and hung from ceiling beams to hold the jars. During the winter, we enjoyed the harvest of Mom's hands very much. Sometimes, however, we would not work our way through all of the jars, and over the years a backlog of certain items might build up. The result eventually would be an occasional jar turned white from waiting for its contents to be consumed. At that point, naturally, the only answer would be to throw away the moldy food. Those aging jars always reminded me of ancient men sitting back and watching their much younger neighbors still bright and spry, while longing for the opportunity to be of use themselves.

The outside bulkhead door to the cellar led down stone steps that could become slippery in winter or even after a heavy rain. In winter, though, we avoided using that entry, instead piling straw bales on top of the door to help insulate the cellar from the cold.

A flight of wooden stairs led from the first floor of our house to the cellar. We used those stairs in the winter and during storms—carefully, I might add, as the stairs were steep and the individual steps not very large. Still, that approach kept us warm and dry as we descended into the cellar to grab another jar of strawberry preserves, beans, or whatever Mom's menu of the day called for.

Edward J. Rielly

A Long Thin Closet and Connections

An unusual closet stretched between two of our bedrooms. It had a door on one end but stood open at the other, a condition my mother addressed by hanging a curtain over the opening. Hooks screwed into one wall accommodated clothes hangers, while other items—shoes, boxes, whatever—piled up on the floor against the walls.

The closet literally was a walk-through closet, a kind of tunnel connecting the two rooms. One of the rooms was my childhood bedroom, just big enough for a single bed and a wooden bookcase that contained books and toys. Pictures hung on the walls, including a black cutout of my profile created at school and a painting of the Virgin Mary. Looking out the single window, I could see the backyard and, beyond the fence, the old tree where our hammock hung in warm weather.

I kept my baseball cards under the bed, at first in a cigar box, and later, as my collection grew, in a much larger box. The room was comfortable and cozy.

Later I inherited the much larger room at the opposite end of the closet—after my brothers had grown up and moved into their own homes. Its window looked out toward the east and the barns and the driveway. With the window open, I could hear, much easier than from my earlier room, those morning sounds of cattle calling from their pasture or a rooster crowing.

This bedroom had a stovepipe, the advantage of which I much appreciated. The larger room held a larger bed, befitting a slightly older and larger me. That bedroom I kept through high school and college, and used when I would return to the farm in later years.

But back to the closet. In a way, it has always seemed like a connection drawing me back to the farm, as it was literally a connection between the two rooms. It connected my early childhood to later years, serving as a type of bridge for my passage from childhood to adulthood. The years I spent growing up on that small dairy farm, living in the old large farmhouse, served me well. They were never years that simply passed by. They remain with me yet, always will. If my early life was a type of long, thin closet, it was a closet stocked with far more than hanging shirts and shoes lined against a wall. My early life was who I was, who I am, who I am still becoming.

It was quite a closet.

Edward J. Rielly

III.
Family Portraits

Some Things, Like Bread Pudding, Last Forever

"Be sure to save room for dessert," my mother liked to say, and I consistently did my best to comply. There were lots of desserts that she was skilled at making, a mouth-watering assortment that included butterscotch pie, devil's food cake, doughnuts (what she called "frycakes") shaken in sugar right out of the boiling oil, and bread pudding. The last one may seem the most pedestrian of them all, but to me it was the epitome of dessert, the ultimate rationale for saving room for what really mattered.

My wife accuses me of associating desserts with love, and I plead completely and unremorsefully guilty. If there were one thing that characterized my mother more than her desserts, it was love. There was never any doubt about that. The moon might fall, the sun might not rise in the morning, the cows in the back pasture of our Wisconsin farm might not heed my father's early summons, but love and desserts would prevail.

How sweet that bread pudding was! A heavy dose of sugar dissolved among the raisins and the bread and the lesser ingredients—the milk and eggs—along with a bit of what my mother always called "oleo" (now known as margarine). My mother, in her way, was something of a rebel to use oleo in dairy country, where anything that competed with good farm butter was almost heretical. What was really unequaled, though, was the cinnamon topping. Warm, it melted into my soul. Cold, it was even better: that cinnamon topping glazed over like frozen lava transformed by some god of delicacies into a river of gastronomical delight.

Walking home the mile from the one-room school I attended, I always looked forward to supper (I never called it dinner until years later when I became urbanized). I anticipated the day's final meal all the more because my lunch had come out of a school lunchbox (festooned with pictures of Roy Rogers) filled with commonplace foods such as apples and peanut butter sandwiches, and maybe a few cookies. For the great desserts that so delighted me, I had to wait for supper, although I

Edward J. Rielly

Here is my family: from left to right Lawrence, Mom, Mary, me, Dad, Joe.

knew they often were being created even as I was absorbing my reading, writing, arithmetic, and history lessons. Sometimes paying attention in school was a real challenge.

One of the questions that required daily resolution was whether we would eat supper before or after milking. The decision usually resulted from how early my father (with some help from me, and in earlier years from my older brothers) could get the pre-milking chores done, and hence how early the milking could be finished. Especially during seasons devoted to fieldwork, when my father would be on our Allis-Chalmers tractor throughout the afternoon, everything got pushed later a bit, including milking—but not supper. On those days, we ate supper before milking to ensure enough energy to get through the lengthened day.

I admit that I preferred those long working days, rather selfishly, because they meant an earlier invitation to Mom's desserts. I found that the taste of cinnamon really stays with a person, even throughout the process of milking. The cows slowly and methodically chewing their cud, as close as cows can come to cow heaven, had nothing over on me, especially after Mom's bread pudding.

Years later, my father dead and the farmland rented out, the barn empty of cows and the milk house deserted by all but an occasional mouse, my wife, our son and daughter, and I would continue to journey back to Wisconsin. We would stay in the old farmhouse in which I grew up. Waking up in my own childhood room, I could hear cows mooing from a neighbor's farm and gaze out the window at fields of tall, swaying stalks of dark green corn and golden oceans of oats. It was almost like being a child again.

And during our visits my mother still liked little better than preparing food for us. It was the same basic food that I had enjoyed as a child: the boiled potatoes with gravy; beef always well done (no pink meat dared show its face on our kitchen table); soft rolls, sometimes with caramel coating on top (what I had come to know long after childhood as "sticky buns," though the store-bought varieties were always a bit deficient to my way of thinking); and, of course, desserts.

My children, to tell the truth, preferred Mom's frycakes, I think because they were especially portable. Each summer when we began our long drive back to Maine, at least two large containers filled with those frycakes went with us. They would have lasted for weeks and still tasted good, but, of course, it was a challenge to reach home with some still uneaten.

My favorite, though, was the bread pudding. Whenever we visited, I made sure that Mom prepared it, and the taste never varied from what I had experienced as a child. Going home was always a little more complete when I could pick up my spoon and dig into a big bowl of pudding. And the next day there was more pudding, with cold cinnamon topping.

My mother has been dead now for years, and another family owns the farm. We go back less often, and when we do it is usually only my wife and me visiting my sister and her family. No one makes bread pudding quite the same way in Wisconsin anymore. The state is poorer for that fact.

However, I have my mother's recipe embedded on the hard drive of my computer and, naturally, on a back-up disk. I take no chances.

Once in a while I print off the recipe, visit our supermarket, and then get to work. I have brought a touch of technology to the process, but the ingredients are the same. So is the result. The taste is permanent. Some things do not change. Fortunately!

And I remember my mother's admonition, which I pass on to anyone eating with us: "Be sure to save room for dessert."

Just in case you would like to try it:

Recipe for Bread Pudding

Pudding:
Mix together:
- 1/2 loaf of white bread
- 2 whole eggs
- 1/4 cup of sugar
- 1/2 cup of raisins
- 2 tablespoons of oleo*
- 1 cup of milk

Grease pan.

Bake about 45 minutes.

Topping:
Mix together:
- 1 cup of sugar
- 3 tablespoons of flour
- 1 teaspoon of oleo
- 1-1/2 teaspoons of cinnamon

Add about 1-1/2 cups of cold water and mix.

Cook on low heat, stirring, until it thickens. Eat!

* another term for margarine

A Real Cowman

Everyone has certain talents, and my father's lay in handling cattle. Today, farmers certainly know much about cows. They get on their computers and discover the exact ounces of feed to give depending on the sum of the square of a cow's legs, or whatever. Science progresses, and chemicals work miracles. Dairy farming has become big business, and I suspect that many a dairy farmer today goes through his entire life without ever wetting his hands with milk unless he spills while pouring it over his cereal.

My dad was no scientist, but he was hands-on, something of an artist with cows, maybe even something of a cow psychologist. He knew each cow's personality. I think that he loved his cows.

Not that he never got angry with them. I occasionally saw him really ripped when a cow stubbornly refused to stand still for the milking machine or just plain refuse to stick its head into its stanchion. But then people get mad at people, too, and often for less of a reason than obstinacy.

Milking was hard work, and it was unrelenting. A dairy farmer had to milk those cows every morning and every evening every day of the year. There were no vacations, no calling in sick, no taking a personal day.

In winter, the cows were already in the barn, but during the rest of the year, my dad would have to summon them from the pasture. I still can hear him calling them, a call that went something like "Come, Boss!" each word stretching far out, reverberating long and deep down the lane, across the gully, and around the bend into the pasture north of the barn—or across the road and up and down the rolling hills of the south pasture. And the cows heard.

They came. They always came, one after another, trudging up the path. They answered the summons, filed into the barnyard, and entered the barn, knowing which door to enter, recognizing their own stanchions. Once in a while, a cow got confused; at those times, things

Edward J. Rielly

could get interesting, as a cow is a big obstacle to overcome when it starts flailing about trying to find where it belongs. But that did not happen often.

Dad kept the cows giving milk in appropriate, money-producing quantities, the result of effective feeding and overall care, and they seldom got sick. He watched over them, took special care when one was ready to deliver a calf, and wasted no time calling a vet on those rare occasions when one did fall under the weather.

When I was little, my job was to carry the milk pails. We did not have lines transporting the milk from the milking machines to a cooler, as many farmers later had. Nor did we have an automatic barn cleaner. We were low tech.

What we did have was the type of machine that hung under the cow, with four cuplike appendages that went over the cow's teats. Once in a while a cow got a little testy when the machine was being attached. A good sharp cow kick would hurt if it connected, but fortunately their legs were not flexible enough to kick sideways, so they usually missed us. Instead they usually connected with the milking machine hanging underneath, sometimes sending it flying.

When the cow had yielded up her milk, the machine was removed, the milk poured into a tall, shiny pail. Sometimes, in winter, when the cows were annually down in their milk, we could get two cows' worth of milk in one pail, but in summer it was one cow per pail. So in summer I had a lot more trips to make.

I can still walk the route in my sleep: from the near vicinity of the particular cow through the gap at the end of the row of stanchions past a manger, through an open pen (which could be closed up with a gate when we needed to put a calf—sometimes a cow with its newborn calf—in it, allowing just enough of a walkway to pass by), and out the door of the barn. Then into the milk house, at which point I poured the milk into a large metal strainer sitting atop a milk can. The strainer caught dirt, pieces of hay, and such, and I had to change the strainer pad often to ensure that the milk would pour through it. I also had to watch carefully to make sure the can did not overflow. When the milk rose to the top, I quickly moved the strainer to another milk can, sometimes while the milk was still pouring through. I became pretty adept at the quick transfer.

Those milk cans were really heavy when full, and they had to be lifted into the cooler, essentially a large box filled with water. The cooler ran on electricity, so the water remained cold unless the power went out. When I was little, I would watch my dad hoist the cans into the cooler, marveling how it took a real swing to get them up, over, and in, and my dad was not a big man.

A milk truck came every morning, after milking was over, to haul away the cans of milk and return our now empty cans from the day before.

Many years later, when Dad was suffering from emphysema and unable to continue milking, we had a sale. It was one of the hardest days of his life. In addition to the cattle, we sold off the machinery, most tools, the leftover hay and corn, even the milking machines.

But it was the cows that he most hated parting with. When a big truck backed up to the barn, and the cows were driven up a chute into it, a large piece of my dad left as well.

He did keep two cows, though. He just had to keep his hand in somehow. Dad bought calves to put on the cows, to use the milk that we no longer sold. Dad bought the calves very young from a neighbor, and when a calf was big enough, Dad sold it. This was not about money. Perhaps the happiest times of the day for him were when he put the calves to nurse. Dad would sit there beside the cows, resting on his milking stool, and watch.

Eventually, one of the cows had to go; then, finally, even the last one. My dad's health deteriorated, and even that small portion of what he once had done so well ended. Dad always took great pride in his work with cows. I still keep a copy of the sale poster from the farm sale on a wall in my backyard screen house. It helps me remember to cherish what I have.

Edward J. Rielly

Too Neat or Not Too Neat

My mother was a contradiction where neatness was concerned. Outside, everything had to be just so. She took great care ensuring that the yard was groomed. The lawnmower therefore was her most valued machine, and I was its regular driver. We had a huge front yard and a moderate back yard. It took the better part of the day to get it all cut, especially because I had to mow around enough trees to stock a small forest and several flowerbeds.

But keeping the lawn neat was insufficient. The grass outside the yard also had to be immaculate. That especially meant the area between the yard and our long driveway. What good was a neat yard if the area right next to it was overgrown in thigh-high weeds? Of course, that reasoning could extend indefinitely, I thought, mowing from our yard to where the sun rose.

The most annoying aspect of cutting the grass outside our yard involved the area outside the back yard, north of the pump. My mother did not like cars parking there, and so she developed a stratagem for keeping them away: a large semicircle of stones painted white. They looked nice and served the purpose, but every time I mowed I had to move each one of those stones—twice! Once before I mowed, and then afterward, making sure each stone ended up in its appointed place.

My mother planted geraniums in the flowerbeds. As with the lawn, she took great care, installing wire fences to keep fuzzy intruders out. She also had a great fondness for old tractor tires, which she painted white and filled with dirt. The geraniums really took to the tires, stretching their dark redness high above the old rubber.

Then there was my mother's preoccupation with how the other buildings looked to anyone who drove in. A board hanging from a barn wall had to be re-nailed immediately. She had a keen eye for the wind-whipped shingle and the cracked windowpane. When paint started to fade out, it was time for a new coat. My dad could live with a hanging board or faded paint, but not my mother.

But inside the house, neatness was another story. I don't mean that the house was a mess. Far from it. My mother did most of the normal things: sweeping, vacuuming, picking up this and that wherever it fell, keeping things that were immediately visible to the naked eye looking nice.

The problem came when a drawer was opened or a closet looked into. Silverware was a disaster. My mother had neither rhyme nor reason to where the little utensils went. Forks with spoons, knives in all four slots of that rubber silverware holder within the drawer. I must have been traumatized by the disorder. To this day, I cannot stand any mixing of utensils. My wife shakes her head in sorrow as I once again move a big fork out of the salad fork slot, retrieve a spoon from among the knives. My life is not in proper equilibrium until I get the silverware settled.

And the closets! Box upon box in the back, floors covered, clothes hanging as disorderly as a group of drunks making their way down a sidewalk. Now I am unable to face the day if a pair of slacks had made its way among the dress shirts in my closet. Yes, maybe I do need therapy.

Covered Wagon

We all know what a covered wagon is. Pioneers went West in covered wagons, hauling the few possessions they deemed most essential to start a new life. Oxen pulled them if the pioneer were smart, horses if he was not, oxen being as slow as molasses but strong and steady. In later years, covered wagons crawled across our theater and television screens.

Like many a child, I had toy covered wagons to go with my cowboys and Indians. I still have some of them. But my favorite covered wagon was the davenport in our living room. We never called it a sofa. Maybe city people did.

My mother played covered wagon with me. She would have me sit close to her, and she would cover our legs with a blanket because, of

Edward J. Rielly

course, traveling across the plains can get pretty cold.

And the sights we would see! My mother was good at pointing them out to me. Deer, buffalo, rivers we might have to cross, a prairie fire, an imposing mountain blocking our way. But we persevered, stopping for an occasional snack. My mother was good at snacks too.

I have a different version for my grandchildren. Technologically advanced, we climb to the stars instead, that new frontier. We sit in my recliner, and I push down the wooden handle sending our feet out straight. Then I push back so that we are just about lying flat, to give us a real sense of being high above everything. We wave to the folks below and fly so very fast from state to state, across the country.

It's just a little updating of covered wagon time, but the principle is the same. Still, how far we have come. My mother and I crossed half the country in a covered wagon. Now my grandchildren and I journey far and high, crossing vast stretches of land but also reaching into the clouds. Maybe, one way or another, we are also heading a little closer to my mother.

The Missed Stop

My Uncle Ray, my father's brother, decided to visit us from Chicago for a week or so. I cannot recall today precisely how long he planned to stay, or exactly how long he did stay. In any case, he was with us one day less than he intended. The reason was a point of controversy.

You see, Uncle Ray fell asleep on the train and missed his stop, not waking up until he hit Dubuque, several stops and some sixty miles from where he was supposed to disembark.

My father had gone to meet him at the train station and was understandably worried when Uncle Ray did not get off the train. Dad wondered what happened, and the rest of us shared that concern after Dad got home.

We found out later that evening by means of a phone call from Uncle Ray. Now Uncle Ray, a thin man without much hair left, could be a bit cranky, and sometimes just a little unreasonable. Yet he was a very good man. He had a heart of gold, as the saying goes. He might get angry and tell someone off, but if a person needed help he was right there for the person.

That night, crankiness took over. From his point of view, the fault for his missing his stop did not lie with his falling asleep, although many people might consider themselves to have some obligation to keep track of where they were, where they were going, and how soon they would get there.

No, for my uncle the fault lay with the conductor, who clearly (didn't we all see it?) should have known where Uncle Ray was to get off and made sure to let him know when the train was approaching his destination. Forget all the other passengers. The conductor should have remembered where Uncle Ray was going, and come back to make sure Uncle Ray was prepared for his stop, and wake him up if he were sleeping. What kind of conductor was he anyway?

None of us attempted to disabuse Uncle Ray of his opinion. As I said, he had a heart of gold. We were happy to have him with us, even if he was somewhat delayed. Among just us, though, we had more than one good laugh about the night Uncle Ray fell asleep on the train.

My Sister

It was my sister, Mary, seven years older than I, who financed the new bathroom in our house, making the outhouse of blessed memory an anachronism quickly dispensed with. Before long, no trace of it remained; the holes were filled in, and grass covered the spot.

Mary was the first member of our family to attend college. She went to Platteville State Teachers College in Platteville, Wisconsin. The institution I believe is now considered the University of Wisconsin at Platteville, or something like that. Mary became a teacher in the days when one could begin teaching with only two years of college. She later finished the four-year degree and had a successful teaching career before

Edward J. Rielly

returning to farming with her husband. Other jobs later came along, but it is of those early years that I speak here.

My sister, Mary, seemed to want a little sister. At least I appear remarkably holy.

Mary was very generous with her salary. In addition to the bathroom, she bought a 1955 black and white Ford that other members of the family also used after she married and left the car with us. I did some of my early driving in that car. Later, after it had run its course, the Ford retired to a back pasture where it sat for decades surrounded by tall weeds, providing a comfortable home to generations of field mice. Mary also contributed hugely to financing my college education. Without her help, I would not have become a college graduate, a teacher, and a writer. In fact, I would not be writing this today. I could be self-deprecating and say that perhaps reading this, Mary may have second thoughts about that long-ago investment, but the truth is that she never has had second thoughts about helping anyone.

Growing up on the farm, Mary found herself also doing a lot of farm work. She drove tractors regularly, which was a job assigned to farm girls then. Men did the heavy lifting. (Political correctness had not yet been born.) There is a photograph of Mary driving our tractor and Dad on the high mower-seat behind, raising and lowering the long sickle. The mower we had then required a rider, so cutting hay, for example, was a two-person job.

Mary's teaching began at a one-room schoolhouse a few miles from the one she and my brothers had attended, and where I was still a student. Our two schools got together a couple of times for a softball game, something of a home-and-home series. It seemed a little strange seeing my sister as a teacher, although she often had been that to me.

I remember a few stories about Mary when she was very young. One has her climbing up on the top of the old-style, wooden wall telephone we used to have. As I remember the story, she adamantly refused to climb down, although finally, she had to. Maybe our mother needed to place a call. Mainly, though, I recall her playing with me. Seven years separated us, so she was definitely my big sister. School was a favorite game, with Mary as teacher, which, as I said, she later became. I suspect that my lifelong interest in education came out of those school games, as I discovered that learning can be fun, which has stood me in good stead these many years.

Mary took a special interest in me from the first, even if she had hoped for a little sister. As soon as our mother returned from the hospital with me, Mary became my special protector, although, to be fair, both of my older brothers also did plenty of protecting, as I point out elsewhere in this memoir. One day our parents went to the village of Waldwick to buy groceries, leaving Mary to babysit. As I slept in my crib, my brothers, Joey and Lawrence, came to check on this new addition to the household. However, Mary thought that they were being too loud and might wake me up. She wasted no time telling them off.

It may have been that secret wish for a sister that induced Mary to play dress-up with me. I retain some photographs of me dressed up like a girl. In one, I wear Mary's First Communion dress and veil. Maybe Mary found that funny. Maybe I should take back some of those nice things I just said about her. I won't, though. Everybody should have a big sister like mine.

Edward J. Rielly

Grandpa McKeon

My Grandfather McKeon died in 1955 at the age of ninety-seven. I remember him as a tall, thin man with gray, thinning hair swept to the right and a big mustache. His hands were large, befitting the baseball player he was as a young man, his hands ideal for grasping the ball. I have heard that he was a catcher, but no corroborating records seem to exist. However, his nickname— "Flicker"—was always assumed in our family to refer to his ability to grab the ball and throw it quickly, certainly a useful skill for a catcher.

Grandfather McKeon and I are enthralled by our first television.

OCT - 54

Grandpa McKeon had outlived his wife, Julia, by about sixteen years when he passed away. From time to time, he came to stay with us for a while. He loved to fish, but we had no stream on our farm, so he spent his time mainly sitting in a rocker chewing tobacco, watching the television that we had recently bought, or both.

He kept a big coffee can beside his chair and spat regularly into it. My mother cleaned it out for him without complaint, though it is unlikely she cared much for the chore. For me, it was fascinating to watch him chew and spit. Not quite as fascinating, though, as television.

Grandpa McKeon and I shared a keen interest in the new television, and we both had enough free time to watch it, one of the advantages of being either very young or very old. Looking back, I guess that he must have been truly amazed at the changes he had witnessed in his life, both technological developments such as the television and the changed world that he saw on the screen.

James Mason McKeon was born on January 1, 1858, in the southwestern Wisconsin town of Kendall, over three years before the beginning of the Civil War. I never thought to ask him the questions that today I would give so much to ask: Do you remember anything of the war? What did you do when as a young man you spent a couple of years in the Dakotas (which were then still a territory)? Where did you play baseball? And I surely would ask him about the mine accident when he was blown safely away while his brother-in-law, John Boyle, was fatally injured. It happened, I know, sometime in the 1890s. Boyle's wife was Mary Ann Fox, my grandmother's sister, the two couples having been married in a double ceremony.

On that fatal day, sparks ignited some dynamite. The explosion burned John Boyle's clothes off, and in agony he raced to the McKeon home. Julia, my grandmother, wrapped him in a white sheet and surely saw to other treatments, although no documentary record of that treatment survives. No doubt a doctor was summoned, but John died a few days later. Yes, I would also like to know more about that.

But most of all, I would like to know what went through my grandfather's mind when he thought back over the years and remembered the enormous changes that had occurred: transcontinental railroads, automobiles, airplanes, freezers and refrigerators, and, of course, the television. And what did he find still the same? Fishing, I suppose. Certainly much of farming, which he had done most of his life, was at least recognizable, even if the equipment had changed, such as horses yielding to tractors and so forth.

I recently reflected on the generations I have known and in some way experienced, in some way been a part of. Between the birth of Grandpa McKeon and the expected life span of my youngest grandchild will be a remarkable stretch of about 230 years. I stand in the middle. So much has changed since my grandfather's birth, and so much more will change during the lifetime of my grandchildren. And I get to be in the center of it all. Of course, so do any number of other people, but that realization does not diminish the awesome sense I feel of being within a huge chunk of history.

Sharing a Mounds

A candy bar may seem inconsequential, something that tastes good but is quickly devoured and forgotten until the next one comes along. It is true that most candy bars meant no more than that to me growing up. But not Mounds candy bars. Or, more precisely, not the Mounds bars that my dad and I shared after a job well done.

The particular job that called for Mounds bars was bringing in the cows for milking from the south pasture. We would walk down the lane leading south from the barnyard, cross the road, open the gate into the pasture, and usher the cows, which usually were waiting for us, back the way we had come. There was no water in the pasture except when a small spring flowed for part of the season before drying up, so the cows were ready for a good drink.

Once the cows were on their way up the lane, they inevitably continued into the barnyard, where they pushed, bumped, and jostled each other on their way to the stock tank.

So my dad and I had some time to kill while the cows got their fill of water. Sometimes, during that wait, Dad would reach into his overalls pocket and pull out a Mounds candy bar for us to share. We would sit down on a grassy bank, and my dad would open the package, and we would each pick out one of the mounds. The chocolate probably was a bit melted, but I cannot recall noticing. After all, a little smeary chocolate never hurt the taste of a candy bar.

The Mounds candy bar, for those unacquainted with the delicacy, consisted of two identical but separate mounds. I always loved Mounds bars and had a ritual for eating one. I would take my mound and carefully eat away the chocolate from top, bottom, and sides, until only a lump of coconut remained. How sweet that coconut tasted as I nibbled away at it! Dad ate the other one, but not my way. He just ate it in normal bites. I guess that was the adult way.

In this modern world of counting calories and watching one's sugar intake, I eat few Mounds bars. But when, on those rare occasions that I do, I cannot resist resorting to my old ritual, first the chocolate, then the coconut. Some things should never change. And I never eat a Mounds bar without thinking of how special it was to share one with my dad.

Mom's Driving (Or Not)

My mother never drove a car or truck when I was growing up. In fact, one of my clearest memories of going to town is of Dad driving the blue Ford pickup, me in the middle, and Mom to my right. The child always sat in the middle. I think that is a law of nature. Being seven years younger than the next youngest sibling meant that often I was the only child going along.

My dad drove slowly. He liked to take in the sights as he drove, seeing how a neighbor's corn was doing, who seemed to be home—anything that appeared interesting. Of course, since Dad liked to observe what was happening to the right and left, he sometimes tended to let the truck veer a bit toward the middle of the road. Fortunately, the gravel roads were not much traveled, and Dad always got the truck back where it belonged before he took the next curve.

But even more than the driving, it is the waiting that I remember. Dad did not have a lot of shopping to take care of in town, as Mom handled most of it. She bought the groceries and just about anything that was not directly animal- or crop-related, such as cow feed or bailing twine. Often I accompanied Mom into the stores, but sometimes I waited in the truck with Dad. Dad did a lot of waiting in the truck, just looking about. If he complained much, it has escaped my memory.

Of course, the fact that Mom did not drive made her dependent on Dad to drive her wherever she wanted to go. I wondered about that once or twice. But mainly I just accepted the way things were.

Yet, I finally learned that there was a story to my mother not driving. As the story goes, she was sitting in our pickup one day when a minor accident occurred that could have been far more serious—but let a poem that I once wrote about the incident tell what happened:

Edward J. Rielly

Why My Mother Wouldn't Drive

There is a legend
in my family about why
our mother would never drive.
It seems one day before
I can remember, maybe
before I was born, she was
just sitting in our pickup
waiting for Dad to return,
parked beside the village
General Store, and the truck
started rolling forward
down a slight incline
gently pushing the store
proprietor, who happened
to be crossing the street,
until he jumped out of the way.

Then Dad saw where she was
going and hurried back
and jumped into the driver's
seat and slammed on the brake.
When he had done all that
he turned to our mother, so
the story goes, and asked her
where she intended to go,
and if she would like to drive
back home, or somewhere else.

That was enough for her. From
that day on she never again
even entertained the idea that
she might learn to drive, decided
that just riding and letting
someone else handle the driving
would do just fine. Still,

Dad never let her forget about
the day she went for a drive
and took a certain man along
for a ride, brief though it was.

I refer to the story as a "legend" because the incident, although true, may not be the actual reason why Mom never drove. I suspect that she never learned simply because she never had to learn and had no particular desire to do so. A lot of women back then did not learn how to drive. The incident that I relate makes for a more entertaining story, though, than someone just never learning. So, to return to the legend, from then on and forever Dad drove, and Dad waited.

Pies

Pies were probably the most common dessert in my family, although cakes, doughnuts (my mother's "frycakes"), cookies, ice cream, candy, and my personal favorite—the previously discussed bread pudding—were common as well. "Save room for dessert," my mother would say, and she meant it. Believe me, I did not need much convincing.

Pies were a great specialty of my mother's. She made pie crust to die for: flaky, tasty, a perfect vehicle for whatever went inside it. What went inside it varied a lot, sometimes coming from our orchard or from our yard, at other times coming from the top of the stove. We had cherry trees and apple trees in the orchard, and they supplied the fixings for many a pie. I retain a special taste for cherry pies, although no one else in my current family cares as much for things cherry. Of course, they did not have the training I had.

Apple pies were common at home as well. They may be the most common type of pie anywhere. Although other pies are sexier, a good piece of apple pie always goes down well.

My mother also baked gooseberry pies and rhubarb pies, thanks to the gooseberry bushes and rhubarb plants growing in the fence line along the western and northern borders of our yard. I liked rhubarb a lot, but gooseberry pies were at the bottom of my list—although I never turned down a piece of any kind of pie. I always found gooseberries a bit sour.

Then there were the pudding pies, especially chocolate and butterscotch. My mother did not simply open a box of instant Jello pudding mix and, a minute later, there was something that looked a bit like pudding. No, she made her pudding from scratch. The chocolate was rich, dark, and thick. I especially loved it cold. Then there was her butterscotch pie. I have had pies since that at least came close to hers, but never someone else's butterscotch pie. The taste was so distinct that I can still savor it decades later. Some tastes never go away, remaining always in that portion of the brain reserved for the most unforgettable tastes. I'm not sure where that spot is located, but it must reside in a portion that God made first, before He settled on where to place lesser functions, like language and muscular control.

My mother's pies, of course, were a great hit with relatives and neighbors, whether consumed in our house or at a neighborhood function. I remember well one time when a great-aunt of mine was visiting. Her name was Alice, and she had lost her ability to speak because of an illness many years earlier. That disability, however, did not keep her from making her wishes known where one of my mother's pies was concerned. She noticed that my mother had placed a pie in the shut-off oven to keep it fresh. Great-Aunt Alice was not able to speak, as in "I would love a piece of that pie," but she communicated clearly enough by pointing at the oven door and making the only sort of sound that she could make, something like "Tah-tah-tah" with a rising pitch. We got the point, and she enjoyed her piece of pie.

My mother never lost her taste for pie, even after she had lost some of her pie-making ability. In later years, whenever she and I would stop into a restaurant, she would always save room for dessert, which is to say, a piece of pie. Even today, I cannot order a piece of pie without thinking of her. In fact, I'm convinced there are some things I do, at least unconsciously, just to be a little closer to my deceased parents, like ordering a piece of pie, or the way I seldom sit behind the steering wheel of my car without remembering my father.

We connect in a lot of ways, such as enjoying a good piece of pie.

"Sit Down and Eat, Irene"

My mother took meal preparation seriously, especially when we were having guests. She planned carefully, made sure that we had picked up enough meat from the locker in town (before our investment in a freezer), and started baking early in the morning, if not the night before. Her work never stopped with food preparation, though, but continued right through the meal.

My mother, in addition to being the cook, was the waitress as well. But she did not merely set the table and place the food on it. She continued to remain upright, bustling about to make sure everyone was eating a lot, having seconds, yet saving room for dessert (there was always room, naturally, no matter how many helpings of potatoes, bread, meat, and so forth that one had eaten), and ensuring that everyone was having a good time at the table.

This eternal bustling was second nature to my mother, but most people dining with us—whether relatives or friends—being decent sorts,

Supper in the Rielly kitchen: me, Dad, Joe, and Mary. Mom, as usual, is not sitting down, in this case, taking the picture.

Edward J. Rielly

quickly grew a little uncomfortable with my mother working steadily instead of sitting down to eat. "Sit down and eat, Irene" became a common utterance during our meals. Mom, however, was adept at deflecting this directive with repeated "I will, now, in just a minute" responses.

One of my uncles by marriage, Uncle Mac, was the absolute best at actually getting my mother to comply. A superficially gruff but always compassionate man, Uncle Mac certainly appreciated the food he was eating, but he also appreciated the effort that went into preparing that food. He knew and sympathized with how hard my mother had been working, and he was not about to allow my mother to continue working while everyone else ate. Thus my mother's attempted deflections simply did not work with him.

So Uncle Mac would rise and escort my mother to the table and gently propel her into her chair. He was one person who could tell Mom to sit down and eat and get her to do it.

Uncle Mac's wife, Aunt Arline, who was one of my father's sisters, usually seemed very serious, a no-nonsense type of person. She could be a bit intimidating, yet she was just as given to empathy as her husband. Years later after the barn belonging to my sister and her husband burned down, a letter arrived in the mail. When Mary opened it, there was a sizable check inside from Aunt Arline. A good heart cares about such important matters as losing one's barn, as well as sitting down at the table to enjoy the food one has prepared.

Summer Cousins

There was considerable difference between my cousins on my mother's side of the family and those on my father's. The former were much older than I, while the latter were close to my age, in some cases the same age. This resulted from my mother being the youngest in her very large family, so naturally her children came along later than those of her sisters and brother. Adding to the difference in age was that I was the youngest in my family by seven years. That made me the youngest in the

Johnny Gavagan, one of my Chicago cousins, and I dare a close-up with our cows in the barnyard.

JUL • 54

very large group of cousins in my mother's family. Some of my maternal cousins, in fact, were old enough to be my mother or father.

The upshot of this was that I did not get to know those older cousins very well. Some of them I barely knew at all, as they had moved on with their lives before I was born, so that I seldom saw them except occasionally at a wedding or funeral.

The children of my father's sisters (his two brothers never married and had no children) were close in age but distant in miles, ironically, much more distant in miles than most of those so-much-older cousins. Nonetheless, my father and mother remained close to his family, and that meant that I had the opportunity to interact quite a bit with my cousins on my father's side.

Most of them lived in Chicago, while we lived on a farm in southwestern Wisconsin. Their parents, however, did have vacations, while my father, having to milk cows twice a day, 365 days a year, barely knew what a vacation was. Consequently, we got together on our farm. In fact, several of my cousins would come up to the farm and stay for a couple of weeks during the summer, sort of like going to camp.

My cousins' time on the farm undoubtedly meant a lot more work for my mother, but I recall no complaints from her. We welcomed them.

Edward J. Rielly

I think that my parents seemed to feel that in a way the farm was partly the whole Rielly family's farm, as it was my dad who inherited it from my grandfather, Edward Rielly. (I might here mention that I was named after my two grandfathers: Dad's father and my mother's father, James McKeon. Thus I became Edward James Rielly.)

I enjoyed having my cousins visit us. It was nice to have someone to play with on a regular basis, given my position chronologically within my immediate family and the inevitable isolation that came from living on a farm well out in the country. They spent enough time on the farm to develop some understanding of what farming was about but not enough time to lose that sense of farming fun. Driving a tractor (with my dad or one of my older brothers riding along to avoid a catastrophe) or helping with chores around the barn still seemed like an adventure rather than a chore to them.

Our farm also was a bit like a petting zoo, although a lot of the animals did not particularly go in for being petted. A heavy cow locked securely in a stanchion could be pretty placid about it, but our sheep (actually my sheep) were downright skittish. I remember vividly one of my male cousins chasing those poor sheep wildly throughout our orchard (which also served as a sheep pasture), trying to catch them. He had to be called off eventually in order to protect the sheep from sunstroke.

Climbing our special climbing tree in our front lawn by the gravel road (which I talk about elsewhere in this memoir) was a ritual for my cousins as it was for me—and later for my children and grandchildren. I am sure that each cousin can still remember sitting on a nice fat branch in that tree.

Milking, especially in the evening, was the highlight of the day for my cousins. Everything on a dairy farm revolved around milking, which provided the primary source of income. The fieldwork—disking, plowing, planting, cultivating, harvesting—was primarily to provide food for the cows. Pigs, sheep, and chickens were secondary part-time jobs, important in supplementing income and providing food. The sheep were my way of making money while city kids were working in stores, pumping gas, and so on.

The process of milking elicited a lot of interest from my cousins. Of course, each cousin at some point tried his or her hand (not to sink too far into punning here) at milking a cow without the aid of a milking machine. Fortunately, we were many years removed from milking cows by hand. Our herd was modest in size by today's standards—a couple dozen milk cows—but even that number would have kept us there most of the night without the help of modern technology.

I cannot ever remember, though, any cousin helping to clean out the barn. I guess that shoveling manure did not seem quite so exciting as getting a cow to give up its milk.

Well, we had a good time, and nobody ever got seriously hurt. These days when I see those cousins, which is not nearly so often, they remember the farm and their visits to it fondly. So do I.

Some Random Images

Memory is the accumulation of images, and a great many of my memories include images from my youth. They constitute the bulk of this book, of course, for what is a memoir but descriptions of images from the past? Here are a few that have not made it into other entries, at least not in any detail.

I think of my mother in the morning, not so much doing what one might expect—preparing breakfast—but walking barefoot in our lawn. You see, my mother had a fair amount of trouble with her feet and found that nothing eased the occasional ache so well as morning dew. She would leave her shoes and stockings off when she got up on summer mornings, and before doing much of anything else she would head out onto the soft, green, moist grass.

When my father came downstairs in the morning, he was always fully dressed, wearing, of course, his overalls. The two clothing items that come to mind so often when I think of my father are his overalls and his ties. They may seem like a strange pair because, of course, they never appeared together. In fact, he wore his overalls far more often, virtually every day. He wore blue and white striped overalls with several pockets and a bib that connected to the back of the overalls with two wide

Edward J. Rielly

suspenders by means of metal clasps that fit down over metal buttons on the bib. I remember the cuffs as well, and how they often had picked up some hay or grain by the time Dad returned from the barn. The overalls were sturdy and enormously practical, what with all those pockets, the ease of dressing in

A bit older, I stand ready for the next bale to come out of the chute, with Dad driving.

the morning, and the rugged, sturdy cloth that seemed never to wear out. Cool, though, they were not. Younger farmers might forgo overalls in favor of blue jeans, which would be a bit cooler, but no farmer worthy of the title would even think about wearing shorts. Of course, in those days, not many males anywhere wore shorts once they graduated from kindergarten.

Yet I also remember Dad's ties. He would wear a tie with his one suit for Sunday Mass and for weddings and funerals. In truth, he did not have a lot of ties—not the dozens that I plead guilty to owning—but the few he did own he must have owned for decades. I never remember his actually buying a tie or, for that matter, receiving a tie as a Christmas gift. What I do see when I think about his ties is their hanging on his dresser. Dad kept them handy and visible, draped over the ends of the dresser mirror. When he needed one, he simply plucked it off his mirror and tied it, looking right into that same mirror to get it right.

I see both my parents at the kitchen table with their pencils out. Mom would be writing letters with a clear handwriting that still today I could pick out from a thousand writing samples. Her spelling and grammar, though adequate, were not great, the result of never finishing grade school, which she left in order to help out on her parents' farm. Later, after going away to college and, still later, moving with my wife and children to Maine, I would receive many letters from her. They were always newsy and enjoyable. And they always brought me back to the kitchen table, even after my dad had died and Mom was living in an apartment in our hometown.

Dad did not go in much for letters, but he worked a lot with numbers, keeping track of milk hundred weights and various other figures relating to our farm. He made his numbers small and visually precise, the kind one makes with a very sharp pencil with a fine point. When he was not figuring on paper, he did so on the inside of the milk house door, especially when making calculations regarding milk production. I wish I had removed that door and kept it before our farm was sold.

So many images come to mind: Dad walking slowly from the house to the barn, or from the barn to the house, the way one walks when tired, or when anticipating another round of hard work; Mom bent over weeding her geraniums; Dad attaching the milking machine to another cow; Mom baking pies or making frycakes at the stove; Dad at the end of the day sitting by the radio in the kitchen, his head leaning into one of his hands, listening to a baseball game; Mom washing the supper dishes in an old dish pan at the sink, gazing through a kitchen window toward the east, perhaps wondering what the next day, and the days after that, would bring.

I have lots of memories of my sister and brothers, too, but being the youngest by seven years in my family, I spent a number of years with my parents after my older siblings had left our farm, moving along the various paths of their own lives. So when I think of the farm and the farmhouse, I primarily remember my parents.

Edward J. Rielly

IV.
Old-Fashioned
School Days

My One-Room Schoolhouse

Many millions of Americans learned their "three R's" (reading, 'riting, and 'rithmetic) in the one-room schoolhouses that once dotted the countryside. They also learned a lot more, from how to contribute toward the common good by taking turns hauling water in from the outdoor pump, to how to focus on their schoolwork amid distractions as older (or younger) students took their turn having class with the teacher.

I was one of those students in the late 1940s and early 50s, the last generation of Wisconsin youngsters in one-room schools before consolidation brought about larger buildings, larger student bodies, and educational changes that, like most changes, had both their good and bad aspects.

My school, Fort Defiance in southwestern Wisconsin, named after a nearby fort long gone, stood in a square lot fronted by a gravel road and surrounded on the other three sides by pastures. A boys' outhouse was located at one end of the playground, the far left as one faced the school, and an identical building for the girls stood at the opposite end, the two facilities as far from each other as the parent-populated school board could place them. An iron pump and a flagpole welcomed us not far from the front door, and a large tree leaned over the boys' outhouse. Somehow the tree was open season for climbing by both boys and girls, despite its proximity to that building reserved for us boys.

The large front playground witnessed many a game of softball and football during warm weather. During winter, we played fox and geese (a kind of tag game requiring us to flee or pursue, depending on which animal we were, along previously marked snow trails) and went sledding down the incline from school to road along one edge of the playground. We played many other games as well. Sometimes we chose up sides for ante-ante-over, a game that involved tossing a rubber baseball over the schoolhouse and then trying to race around to the other side without being tagged. Red rover was an especially physical contest, par-

Edward J. Rielly

ticularly hard on our arms. We lined up in two rows, each side holding hands, while we took turns instructing the other side to send Dale or Rhoda or Karen over, and then held on for dear life to keep that student from breaking through our line. Anyone who could not break through had to join our line, and the game continued until one team captured everyone on the other side—or until the bell sounded ending recess. Even writing about these games gives me the old urge to get up a game of red rover or pull my old bat out of the closet.

The most important activities, of course, occurred inside. All eight grades occupied rows of desks that were firmly affixed to steel runners. No desk moved unless all the desks in that row moved, so no one ever thought about putting desks in circles as I myself often do with my own students today. We stayed put and worked hard at our reading, writing, math, and history. There were not a lot of curricular frills at Fort Defiance. We had opportunities to draw and color, which was art class. For music, we turned on the radio and sang along to an educational program out of Madison. It was called *Let's Sing*—simple and direct, like the education we received.

We had about thirteen students in the school during most of my eight years there, but my class was the large one. We had three students: Karen Cline, Jerry King, and me. Sometimes the teacher (always a woman during my schooldays) put classes together to make handling eight classes and several subjects in one day doable. Whatever the exact composition of our group, when it was our turn for a subject, we moved to the front of the building, onto a stage, and sat around a table with the teacher. Everybody else, of course, could hear what we were doing, so by the time I reached eighth grade I had already progressed through every subject and each grade quite a few times. That has always struck me as one of the benefits of one-room education. Another was the individual attention from the teacher, who might not have been as formally educated as most teachers today but who made up for it with dedication, hard work, and real caring. My sister, by the way, taught in a similar school a few miles away.

Christmas was the best season, not just for the long vacation, but also because we always put on a Christmas program for our families. A thick paper curtain rolled down from the ceiling, shutting the stage off from the rest of the building. The only times I can remember using it were for the Christmas pageants. All of us, of course, participated, depending on our talents. Our parents always seemed to feel that we children had extraordinary gifts of the musical and dramatic sorts. We sang carols as a group and acted out scenes from the Nativity story. The birth of Jesus and the annual visit of Santa Claus vied for top billing in our programs.

At five, when I was in what would later be formalized as kindergarten, I recited the poem "The Night Before Christmas"—a dramatic achievement that I have never surpassed. I looked out at my family and neighbors sitting on chairs or squeezed into children's desks and concentrated on remembering my lines. In those days, even a one-room schoolhouse seemed really big.

I later went on to earn a Ph.D. in English and write lots of books, but I learned my basics right there in that small building. Not long after my eighth grade graduation, the school shut down, merging with several other one-room schools in a multi-room building a few miles away. A family bought my school and moved it into my hometown of Darlington, using it as the basis for a house. Whenever I return, I still drive past the house. If I pull my car over to the side and listen carefully out the open window, I can almost hear the click of a radio knob and a distant voice announcing, "Let's sing!"

So Let's Sing

Singing was an important part of my childhood. Although we never engaged in family songfests around a piano as some families did, I had many enjoyable experiences with song, both at home and at school.

First, though, school. Our one-room school, as I said earlier, had only one teacher to teach about thirteen students who were spread over eight grades. She taught what she could, which was all of the basics. Sometimes there was a little extra as well, if not always formally. There

Edward J. Rielly

was no organized physical education class, for example, though we got plenty of exercise playing during recess and at noon.

Song was somewhere between the more teacher-directed disciplines such as reading and arithmetic and the self-directed physical exercise. The teacher was involved, and we did our singing inside the classroom, but she did not do much actual teaching.

Our singing took two forms. Occasionally, we just sang, using songbooks kept in the piano bench. The teacher played the piano and we sang along. We had the opportunity to choose songs, and being the only student with an Irish heritage, I naturally chose Irish ones. My favorite was number 43 (or maybe 44) in the book, "Wearing of the Green," an Irish ballad from the end of the eighteenth century. The song laments the folks being hanged by the British for daring to wear green and includes such harsh epithets as "England's cruel red" and "the cruel cross of England's thralldom." Some of the other students were at least part English but did not seem to take offence.

Formal music instruction came through the radio, the most high-tech object in the classroom. A Madison, Wisconsin, radio station, WHA, took up teaching music and other subjects to rural schoolchildren as early as the 1930s. The station featured a Professor Edgar B. "Pop" Gordon, who had been expanding listeners' ability to appreciate music since 1922. The station aimed its Wisconsin School of the Air educational programs especially at the approximately 6,500 one-room schools that once dotted the Wisconsin countryside. Pop Gordon remained on the air until 1955 with his *Journeys in Musicland*, and after his retirement Norm Clayton and Lois Dick continued it, changing the title of the program to *Let's Sing*.

My best memories of the program are from after its transformation. There was something really appealing about turning on the radio and hearing the call "Let's Sing."

Songs also were important to me at home, especially those on some of my favorite television programs. One such series was *The Howdy Doody Show*. Buffalo Bob would ask the kids in the studio and those watching at home what time it was. Then the kids in the Peanut Gallery on the set and we watching at home on our black-and-white televisions just before supper (television programming in those days started about 5:00 p.m.) would sing the Eddie Kean lyrics that supplied the answer: that it was Howdy Doody's time. And, of course, we would sing the rest of the song as well, exulting in our sharing that time with Howdy and his television pals.

I was about six when the show, which had begun in late December of 1947, changed its name in 1949 from *Puppet Theater* to *The Howdy Doody Show*. It was still a bit later when we got our first television and I started watching the show. I liked Buffalo Bob, the host, just fine, but my favorite characters were Howdy Doody and the clown, Clarabell, who ran around honking his horn and shooting people, primarily Buffalo Bob, with his seltzer bottle. One of my prized possessions was a Howdy Doody puppet, which somehow got lost during my journey into adulthood.

Another television show that gave me one of my favorite songs was *The Mickey Mouse Club*. I was older, entering into adolescence, when the program premiered in 1955. Monday was Fun With Music Day, as each day had its own special theme (Guest Star Day, Anything Can Happen Day, Circus Day, Talent Round-Up Day), but every day was a day for singing the show's anthem, which asked the identity of the leader of our special television club. The response spelled out the answer in song: Mickey Mouse. The conclusion to the song, sung daily at the end of the show, rather sadly informed me that it was time to say goodbye but affirmed lasting friendship and assured everyone that we would see each other again soon. A million lonely kids who thought they did not have a friend in the world must have reveled in this vast association of friends—an association, and program, alas, that endured only three years.

Such were some of the songs of my youth.

Edward J. Rielly

Kitchen Walls

Most people wallpaper their kitchens or paint them. Either approach can turn out fine, and with the amount of space taken up by cabinets, windows, tall appliances, and hanging utensils, there often is not a lot of wall space to worry about anyway.

Our kitchen was different, though. First, because we really did have a lot of wall space, and second, because my mother had a different approach to decorating those walls. To be completely truthful, the walls were wallpapered, but that was almost unnecessary because she filled much of the space with another type of paper: my school homework.

Just about anything that I brought home from my one-room school—pictures gaudy with bright crayon colors, careful printing along lined worksheet paper, arithmetic problems, a youthful story, a social studies report—went up on the walls. It's not that my mother was insufficiently discriminating about my work, for the fact is that I was a topflight student, which I admit even at the risk of sounding vain. The work, given whatever grade I was in at the time, was usually pretty good.

Nor was my mother just trying to camouflage a bad choice in original wallpaper. She was proud of my work and wanted to encourage me. Having been unable to go beyond the sixth grade herself because of her family's need for her help on their farm, she knew what she had missed and subscribed to that common parental desire to see one's children go farther in life than the parent had managed. So just about everything went up on the walls.

Nor was my schoolwork hidden away in a room seldom seen by any but the immediate family. Our kitchen was the primary room of the house, much more than the living room or the parlor. Our kitchen was the real living room, for it was there that so much of our living occurred. We ate our meals around the kitchen table. My dad spent his evenings after milking bent over beside a radio in the kitchen, head resting in a hand, listening to a Chicago White Sox or Milwaukee Braves baseball game in the kitchen. The radio resided immediately below our wall telephone—our only telephone, of course, long before extensions, cordless contraptions, cell phones, and something called "smart phones." Telephone conversations took place, therefore, in the kitchen, but so did most conversations, within the family and with visitors.

The kitchen was where we received our guests. The most honored spot was right inside the north door, the door we almost always used, where the Morris chair stood. This ancient wooden chair, with handy compartments to the left and right for gloves or anything else we wanted to store, was the kitchen throne. Men especially seemed to love sitting in it. Today it resides with me. I sit in it. I also talk about it at greater length earlier in this memoir.

So guests also got to see my school endeavors. And all of this was with the total approbation of my father, who, like my mother, had been required to cut short his formal schooling (in his case after about two years of high school) for the call of farm work on his parents' farm. Like Mom, Dad very much appreciated educational opportunities and did everything he could to encourage me. That included driving me to school in bad weather, always in our pickup, and even serving for years on our local school committee.

Their efforts worked. Several college degrees, including a doctorate, and too many years of teaching to count, prove how smart they were. What they did worked quite effectively—the power of parental love and kitchen walls.

Some traditions, as I point out here and there within these pages, need to be kept alive. Our children also saw much of their schoolwork go up on our kitchen walls. Now the grandchildren have their turn. To me, a kitchen is not a kitchen without a lot of school papers to make it shine.

Sick Days

Few people like to be sick. Yet there are some exceptions, especially children. Not, of course, throwing-up, fainting-away, weak-as-a-kitten sick. Just sick enough to stay home from school and spend the day in bed or on the couch being pampered.

I did not miss many days of grade school, but once in a while I had one of those not-too-sick days. Just sick enough. I remember them with pleasure. I might try one again someday, but I fear that my wife would not pamper me the way my mother did.

Somehow toast tasted very special on those days. My mother would not give me anything real heavy to eat, but white toast still warm from the toaster and evenly buttered tasted so good! It's funny how something you have thousands of times, often exactly the same way, tastes better within a certain context. Propped up in my bed with extra pillows behind me, I was more than ready for my breakfast toast. There was other food, too. A bowl of oatmeal with a heaping spoonful of sugar and some milk complemented the toast nicely. The cereal also tasted better when Mom delivered it to me in my bedroom than if I had been applying the sugar and milk myself in the kitchen.

In addition, there were special toys saved just for my sick days. Two sets: one of farm animals, the other of tiny metal soldiers. My mother kept them somewhere out of sight. I still have no idea where she hid them. But she kept them hidden successfully, waiting to brighten my sick days. I think that the farm animals, plastic and good-sized, were in a bag; but the toy soldiers lay on cotton in a long, thin, shallow box. I remember that box well. I enjoyed playing with the pig, the dog, the horse, and the rest; but the soldiers were even better. Most of my toys—cowboys, Indians, pirates, and such—were plastic. But these toy soldiers were metal: solid, heavy, and finely detailed.

A sick day was also good for comic books, and if I were even less sick, I would lie downstairs on the couch. That brought television into the equation. We had only one television. In fact, I cannot recall a single family that had more than one when I was growing up. Television was a family affair, a method of uniting, the way radio used to be. There were not a lot of channel choices, usually about three, but television was new and exciting, and we never complained of too few options.

Those were good days to be a little sick. In fact, I feel a headache coming on right now. Where is my wife?

Euchre Evenings

Once a month, Fort Defiance School was the scene of a community gathering that included food, conversation, and euchre. The conversation did not mean a lot to me, but the other two components certainly did.

Each family brought a dish for the potluck dinner. Some brought a casserole, some a dessert, some sandwiches. We brought tuna fish sandwiches—every single time. The reason was because these socials were held on Friday evenings, and in those days Catholics were not permitted to eat meat on Fridays. Fish was not considered meat. That seems a dubious distinction, but a theologian could undoubtedly clear up the matter. Why we brought tuna fish sandwiches, though, was abundantly clear. I was the only Catholic in my thirteen-student, one-room school, and my family was the only Catholic family in the neighborhood.

There was a time before I was born when religious discrimination seriously existed in our Wisconsin community. A local group of the Ku Klux Klan would burn crosses on a hill overlooking our farm. Nothing else happened, though, and by the time I came along, religious toleration had won the day. Even if another child sometimes teased me about my religion, our food contribution testified to that improved tolerance and acceptance. Our Friday diet was accepted as a given fact, one that elicited no negative comments, no snide observations. We were who we were, and our neighbors were fine with that.

The potluck dinner is one of humankind's greatest inventions, right up there with polio vaccine and the internal combustion engine. It was a

Edward J. Rielly

true potpourri of tastes, ready to mingle in a heavenly mix on my plate. If I liked, I could add the desserts right on top, a double-decker. Mainly, though, I preferred to go back for dessert, as long as the best choices were not snatched up too quickly.

The euchre contest also was a monthly delight. We played turn-up euchre as opposed to bid euchre. There may be another name for turn-up, but if so, I never heard it. The version received its name from the practice of turning up the top remaining card after each player had received five cards. The turned-up card would determine the first choice of trump, unless all four players passed and the dealer turned down the card, permitting other players in turn to name the trump.

Names were drawn out of a hat to determine partners and the tables where the players started. Participants had three goals: win games, move from table to table, and rack up a high number of total points. The three goals were related. The winning team at table three progressed to table four, and so forth. Losers stayed put. However, partners changed, so two great card players could not clean up together all evening.

Prizes were awarded. The person with the highest point total for the evening won a prize. The lowest scorer received the booby prize. The former would be something inexpensive but useful, the latter humorous. I wish that I could remember examples, but they escape me. The competition featured another prize or two as well, but memory also fails regarding what they were awarded for. I think that one name was drawn at random, and another may have gone to the person with the most successful lone hands, but I remain unsure.

Going alone and making it was the ultimate euchre thrill. If you judged your hand strong enough, you could decide to play it alone. That meant it was just you versus the two opponents. Four points awaited the successful outcome, one point if you got three or four tricks. The ultimate embarrassment was to play it alone and be set, which meant you pulled in fewer than three tricks. Not only did you fail to get any points, but the opposing team received two. I made it alone a lot of times, and I never suffered the indignity of being set when playing it alone.

Once or twice, I won the grand prize for the most total points. Being in grade school and beating all of those adults, including the table whackers, really felt good.

My father played euchre, but my mother never did, choosing to visit with those other women who chose not to play (although a lot of the ladies did play), and also, while visiting, to keep enough coffee made and things generally tidy.

For all the times I played euchre when I was growing up, I seldom have played since. It is part of my youth, like sledding down snow-covered hills and playing baseball against a high barn wall. Anyway, it would not feel the same playing euchre someplace other than in a one-room schoolhouse.

St. Valentine's Day

St. Valentine's Day was always special at Fort Defiance School. We did not have regular art classes there, but on this special day we got out our colored construction paper, scissors, and paste, and started creating.

First came the valentine box, typically a shoebox with a slit cut in the top through which we would insert our valentines. We covered the box with white tissue paper and attached small hearts that we scissored out of red paper. A little white paste on the box kept the hearts firmly, if sometimes a little lumpily, in place.

Then we got to work on our valentines. Some of the students purchased valentines, small ones with cute, provocative statements such as "Be my Valentine." Maybe a cuddly dog appeared on the card. One had to be very careful about the sayings on the cards, keeping in mind the recipient, especially if the recipient were of the opposite sex. We did not want to convey a message that we might wish to take back.

The best cards, though, were the ones we made. Looking back, I know that they were not all that artful, not especially creative, and fairly repetitious. Red hearts, perhaps some smaller hearts attached in a concentric pattern. White fringe or a white square onto which the red heart was pasted could be made from white lacy paper. That paper must have a name, but I cannot remember it. I remember, however, considering it just about the most beautiful paper I had ever seen. One could, of

Edward J. Rielly

course, keep adding layer on top of layer: red hearts, more white lacy paper, a bigger rectangle of red paper, and some white fringe.

Maybe we were a bit creative after all.

All good teachers keep parents in mind, and our teacher did as well. So we made valentines to take home for parents and siblings. Funny, that word *sibling*. They were just sisters and brothers growing up.

So our family valentines went home, and those for schoolmates went into the decorated shoebox. On Valentine's Day the shoebox was opened, and we received our valentines. I always looked closely to see what that special girl offered as a message, engaging in some careful— and hopeful—critical interpretation.

Spelling Bees

The spelling bee was an important part of our Fort Defiance curriculum. Of course, since there were only about thirteen students in my grade school most of the time during my eight years, the competition was limited in number and I faced the same students many times in these contests. My class was the large one, numbering three, but other grades might be added to the mix, often including grades six through eight.

The process was simple enough. We stood in a line, were given a word to spell, and did so (or not, as the case might be). So long as we kept spelling words correctly, we remained standing. The last one up was the winner.

I was a very good speller but not the only accomplished student in the school. Karen Cline, a blond girl and fine student, proved especially challenging to outspell.

Memory is selective and subjective, so I cannot be sure that everyone enjoyed the spelling bees. The students who tended to miss a word early may not have been all that keen on the exercise. I know that I liked participating, although the tension could get pretty high, especially when something more than a victory in that particular bee was at stake.

A Christmas song at Fort Defiance School.
Karen Cline, my chief spelling opponent, is to my left.

Wisconsin gave great attention to spelling bees, with each county holding its own competition to see who would go on to the state event. The state winner would compete in the national spelling bee. So when our spelling bee was conducted to see who would represent Fort Defiance in our Lafayette County bee, the pressure was on.

As I recall, I represented my school in the county bee when I was in grades seven and eight. To get there, I had to win in my school, and that meant outspelling my schoolmates, especially Karen. I no longer recall whether my closest call came in grade seven or eight, but I remember sweating the outcome when we were down to the final two—Karen and me—and I missed a word.

Now, when the spelling bee competition was reduced to two finalists, missing a word did not automatically remove the student from the contest. The next student had to spell the missed word correctly and then correctly spell the following word. Fortunately for me, Karen slipped up as well, giving me another chance. Second chances are great if they yield positive results, and mine did. Ultimately, I prevailed and moved on to the county bee, which was held in Darlington.

I did all right in the county spelling bee, spelling several words correctly, but I did not win. I was okay with the result, though, as I was up

Edward J. Rielly

against a lot of students, including some from schools with a whole lot more students than little Fort Defiance had.

Looking back from the perspective of an educator, which I have been for decades, I am not sure that those spelling bees were such a great idea. It can be really embarrassing for a student to misspell a word very publicly, especially if a student regularly goes out early. At the time, though, I was mainly thinking of myself. And I enjoyed winning.

Cleaning the Schoolhouse

Students usually look forward to the end of the school year, and I was no exception. In fact, the whole community celebrated the end of the year with a community picnic and a softball game involving students and parents. It was funny watching some of those old folks, probably all of thirty-five or forty, try to play our métier. Certain adults were a bit stiff in their running, and their throws were not so fluid, certainly not up to the high standards that we imagined ourselves to have reached. Somehow an adult swinging at a pitch and missing elicited a smile that no one would have seen on our faces when we did the same.

Then came summer. But my family had one more school-related function: cleaning the schoolhouse. My father chaired our school board for many years, which probably is why we got that task. Strangely enough, I loved helping.

It was work, make no mistake about it: washing the tall windows inside and out, sweeping, dusting, washing the blackboards, scrubbing the water bubbler, making sure nothing remained in any of the desks. We spread some sort of reddish cleansing powder on the wooden floor and then swept it up, leaving the floor clean enough, as the saying goes, to eat off it.

I think that what made cleaning the school fun was the sense of owning that building where I spent so much time. I felt in control. I could go anywhere, look in any corner. I was king of the schoolhouse. Maybe my destiny as a teacher was set in those early summer days helping to clean our school. As a teacher, I would be in charge of my own classroom, even when other people were in it.

So we cleaned up after nine months of hard schoolwork, getting the school all ready for the next year. The building stood closed for those summer months, always appearing ill at ease, incomplete, without anyone there. We drove by it a lot, since we lived just one mile away.

By the time fall rolled around, the other kids and I were ready to return, if not for the academics (though I always enjoyed that part of school), then for the camaraderie. We lived on farms, had a lot of fieldwork to do in the summer, and did not get to spend much time with our friends. So we were happy enough to head off for another school year.

Edward J. Rielly

V.
Handling
Childhood

Just Me and the Barn

Growing up on our farm in southwestern Wisconsin, youngest by seven years of five children, I was always an energetic hike or bicycle ride away from our nearest neighbors. So as baseball came early into my blood, circulating ceaselessly through arms and hands created for nothing so much as swinging a bat or throwing a ball, my isolation set up problems higher than even an outfield fence. But not so high as an old red barn on our farm, and that helped me solve my problem.

A baseball game needs players, but imagination can fashion those players as it will. And above all, I learned to make do with what I had, which is to say the barn, my bat, a rubber baseball that bounced much better than a real one, and some quick hands and feet.

My favorite team was the Chicago White Sox of my 1950s youth, and my favorite player was Nellie Fox, the second baseman. I especially became Nellie, but out of necessity I also had to be everyone else.

It went like this: I marked home plate in the dirt, facing the barn, just where the dirt and grass met the driveway that ran behind me. Still farther behind was a grassy slope leading up to the fence that enclosed our yard. The home plate, by the way, doubled as first base. The other bases existed entirely in my imagination, with no physical counterpart.

The White Sox usually were the home team, so the opponent batted first. I would stand by home plate, bat in my left hand, ball in the right, and throw the ball barnward, aiming it so the rebound brought the "pitch" over my home plate. Quickly I shouldered my bat and prepared to swing. Sometimes, of course, the pitch would be off, and the umpire in me would call a ball. If I misjudged and missed with my swing, I obviously had a strike. Sometimes a rut in the ground caused a crazy bounce that sent the ball at the last second over the plate, so I would call a strike. Unless fooled I swung at anything reasonably good, and usually the ball subsequently banged off the barn wall.

Having now been pitcher, umpire, and batter, I dropped the bat and instantly became a fielder. If I caught the ball on the fly, the batter, of

Edward J. Rielly

course, would be out, victim of a fly ball to the outfield. If the ball bounced, I would field it—as the second baseman, shortstop, or third baseman, depending on where I handled the ball—and fire to first by way once again of the barn wall. With my foot on first base (the former home plate), I speared the ball coming off the wall and chalked up another out. Once in a while, sad to say, I would make an error, and the runner would be safe.

Sometimes, of course, the ball soared beyond me for a hit, the distance it traveled determining a single, double, triple, or home run. A double, for example, passed the driveway and reached a line of decorative rocks painted white by my mother to keep cars off the grass outside the yard. A triple landed just this side of the fence, but if the ball went over or through the fence, reaching our yard, the hitter rejoiced in a home run.

Looking back, I remember that the White Sox usually won. I do not think, honest fellow that I was, that I deliberately "threw" games when batting for the Yankees, Indians, or whichever team was visiting that day. But somewhere down in my deepest desires there must have been a force withholding a slight portion of power at the plate, or perhaps making Nellie and "Little Looie" Aparicio a bit more dexterous in the field than the opposing team's counterparts.

There were many other rules and regulations that I followed. It was essential in my mind to bat as the actual player did, right if right handed, left if left. Nellie was a lefty, so I worked hard at learning how to bat that way. Then there was the high blow over the very top of the barn. I saw no solution other than to call it a home run, but I passionately hated that type of hit and did my best to keep the ball this side of the barn. The reason was the almost always muddy (and, of course, much more than muddy) barnyard. No one wants to wipe all that off his new white ball. With Aparicio as my shortstop, I also learned to factor in stolen bases. Then, as the catcher, I would fire the ball to second (as always off the barn wall), catch it, and apply the tag. For a great runner like Looie to be out, the peg would have to be just so, right at the top of my feet, and my catch clean and the tag swift. He seldom was thrown out.

I spent countless hours at these baseball games and would not trade that experience for all the Little League contests in the world. It has been over fifty years since my last time at bat, and the farm is no longer in my family. The painted rocks are gone, as is the fence. But the driveway is still there, and so is the barn. So maybe some nice evening when the moon is full, and the owners are away, I will sneak back there with my bat and ball and have another game. I will leave a note for my grandchildren with the address of the nearest jail, just in case.

Playing My Cards Right

I still have my baseball cards from the 1950s and '60s—literally thousands of them. Rookie Hank Aarons, MVP Mickey Mantles, Batting Champion Stan Musials, along with the Tom Borlands, Dave Popes, and Carroll Hardys. This is my retirement fund, I say jokingly, almost sadly at times, for, in truth, it almost could have been.

Alas, I dared to exhibit in my youth absolutely no sense of baseball cards as investments. Instead I collected them, kept them (a wise move), but also played with them (not so wise), and wrote on many of them (very unwise indeed).

First, the playing. I had this game whereby I would stage surrogate baseball games with the cards, using them as players around a makeshift diamond on a rug or bed top. To determine whether a player made an out, managed a single, stroked a home run, and so forth, I used the card numbers on the cards not engaged in the game. So if the game were between White Sox and Yankees, all cards for other players would supply the numbers. Take, for example, the number on the back of the 1961 Chris Cannizzaro Topps card: 118. If Minnie Minoso were at bat, and the next card I drew from the pile were this card, I would use the relevant number, the final one, the 8. The 8 would mean a triple for Minoso. A 9 would have given him a home run. Lower numbers would have led downward to a double, a single, or an out, with certain options for double play or strikeout.

Edward J. Rielly

All of this was great fun, especially during inclement weather. One of the advantages was that I needed nothing beyond the cards to play the game, although, as I recall, I usually had paper and pencil to keep track of the action as the game progressed. Playing with my cards in this way was not smart from a financial-investment standpoint, for it inevitably led to rounded corners and occasionally a lasting crease.

The larger proof of my lack of economic forethought was my writing on the cards. I always have been in love with baseball statistics, although my skill at memorization was sharper in my youth. Given this interest, it made sense to me at the time to keep updating the statistics on my cards. So when a new season ended, I would take out my Willie Mays or Ted Williams (yes, I can hear the gasps from those reading this heinous admission) and write the new set of statistics below the old. And I wrote in ink.

So there you have it. My cards remain in all their corner-folded, statistically updated glory—constant reminders of enormously enjoyable (and financially wasteful) years of playing baseball in and out of season. Yet I do not think, even now, with a book before me detailing current prices of baseball cards, I would do it differently. There are other types of investments even more vital than those measured in dollars.

The First Haircut

I am not sure precisely how old I was when I got my first haircut, but I believe about three. That also is how old I look in a picture that I have in a montage on my bedroom wall. I still had long hair then, but it soon came off.

Let me tell you about that picture first. I am in the front with my mother directly behind me. My sister stands to my mother's left, and one of my older brothers, Lawrence, stands to her right, his hands in his pockets. My right hand is raised in a wave, and I apparently am ready to dash toward the camera. My mother and sister, both staring forward, have a firm hold on me. My left arm stands straight up, grasped in my mother's right hand; my sister's right arm angles across my chest. Both my mother and sister evince a remarkable ability to retain their composure while anchoring me within the borders of the photograph.

If the photograph is to be believed, I must have been something of a pistol at times. I surely was during my first haircut. My memory is hazy here; I remain uncertain what I actually remember versus what I have been told countless times. In any case, I was seriously disinclined to have my long blond locks shorn. I have seen many a sheep sheared, and few of them liked it either. Shearers, though, are adept at holding the sheep in a grip that admits little wriggling. Barbers are less trained in the martial arts, expecting some modicum of docility on the part of their sheep. So when I was put in that high revolving chair, I gave the barber a tussle he was unaccustomed to handling.

Scissors and combs do not go well with a squirming child, and the barber, apparently fearing a sharp poke to my eye, was about ready to yield the field when a much older cousin of mine stepped in. We, and virtually everyone else, called him Buddy. Buddy had the solution: a long, thick, red and white peppermint stick, one of those big ones you cannot find anymore.

I'm not sure how long I mulled over the offer, but I did accept it eventually. It must have tasted great. It certainly did the trick. When I left the chair, I had a real boy's haircut, for the first time. There is much to be said for a good bribe.

Annette Funicello

There is a first love for everyone. Or at least I think that's the case. For me, she was Annette, the beautiful, dark-haired star of *The Mickey Mouse Club*. I rushed home from Fort Defiance School every afternoon to watch it; more specifically, to watch her.

The Mickey Mouse Club was a good show, with singing, dancing, dramatic episodes, and a theme song that just grabbed you, although probably adolescents today would fall down laughing at it, times being what

Edward J. Rielly

they are. The members of the show daily asked us in song to name our club's leader. It was a bonding moment, assuring us that we belonged. We, watching from our living rooms on our small black-and-white televisions, knew the answer, of course, and proved our scholasticism by spelling out the name of the mouse with big ears. But it was not Mickey Mouse who summoned me.

Nor was it Jimmie Dodd, one of the co-hosts, or Darlene, or Cubby, though they were among my favorites on the show. It was Annette. Dark-haired with the strikingly dark eyebrows and the big smile. Wow!

I cut a picture of her out of a magazine and pasted it inside the front cover of one of my schoolbooks. It was my favorite classroom text, although I can no longer remember which one it was.

A rumor arose at one point that Annette had been killed in some sort of accident. I did not believe it, refused to believe it. Fortunately, the story proved to be only a rumor, and my world moved forward after holding its cosmic breath.

I was eleven when *The Micky Mouse Club* debuted on television. I was fourteen when it went off the air. The show hit me just at the right time. I was on the road to teenhood, and with a school that included only thirteen students counting myself, there were not a lot of girls around. Certainly not with glistening dark hair, enchanting eyebrows, and such a smile. Annette could sing and dance too. In later years, she released albums and made movies. I bought one or two and saw a couple of her films, sort of for old time's sake, but by then the great romance was over.

But that was another Annette anyway. The one I knew, that one that enchanted me, still wore those big floppy mouse ears. She would sing at the end of the show that it was time to say goodbye, adding, though, that we all would remain friends forever.

You bet!

Trees

Trees were some of my closest companions in childhood. One reason is that I was the youngest by seven years of the children in our family, so I had no one close to my own age as a playmate. And, of course, as a farm boy I did not exactly run next door to share time with a friend. So I made do.

Partly, I made do with trees. A row of four large pine trees stood at the southern edge of our front yard near the gravel road that ran past our farm. They were old then, and remain in place today, older, a bit less full, but still there, except for one of them. The most westerly of the four was very special. It was our climbing tree.

Actually, I never climbed high in it. No one did. But a few feet off the ground, three fat branches reached out from the trunk, providing ample sitting room. The intersection of the branches stretching south and west was my special place. It could be almost anything, like the cockpit of an airplane, a secret hideaway, whatever I wished to make it.

The climbing tree was a place of refuge, and I spent many hours in it. My mother periodically snapped pictures of me and of other members of my family in it, including our city cousins when they came to visit. Later, we took pictures of my children climbing in that tree, or more specifically, posing in that same special seat. It is possible to trace the chronology of two generations of Rielly children growing up in pictures featuring the climbing tree.

Climbing a Pine Tree

We climbed the huge, sprawling pine
that predated by a century the white, two-porched,
colonnaded house my ancestors bought after they
migrated from Ireland. Older than the farm that gave life
to generations of my transplanted family,
it stretched back beyond the long vanished fort down

Edward J. Rielly

the road, to the last battles Indians fought
for survival in that part of the country.

That pine we climbed even before we could walk,
my mother holding a child like a doll
on a limb stretching out straight as an arm pointed
toward the west, toward the dazzling evening sun,
and the child barely able to hold his head up,
and the wind closing his eyes, slipping through hair,
in its way as gentle as the mother.

I came to that pine last, when my brothers had grown out
of that sort of climbing, and only my sister and I
still cared for it, she playing games of trees
with me because there was no other child her age.
By myself, when she went off to school,
I would stand in the center where three large shafts
grew up and out, and where I could grow tired
and lean backward without fear of falling.

Even in my best of days, I never climbed much higher.
It was not a tree for scaling heights,
for daring ventures, for risking arms and legs
to struggle far above one's reach. I would crawl out,
though, along that straight arm of a limb at times
and sit and balance and think of risks. Mainly,
though, I contented myself with the sturdy trunks
of things, hid out between my wooden trinity,
and prayed through small realities, like cones that grew
in multitudes, and that, if flung just right,
would whiz through air with just a trace of sound
and curve gracefully across the road, into the ditch.

Then grown, for years I would bring my children back
for climbing of their own. I would stand beside
the tree, my wife would peep through her small camera

and press a button, and we would add the photo
to the history of our children growing up.

Only now, when my children too have finished
climbing, I realize it was as much the tree's history
being written as our own. The long string of children
climbing this safe and sturdy tree
just proved true what I had suspected:
that there are things in this world that never change,
that dreams prove best that are thick and strong,
that wind loves better than human praying,
and what gives us most gives just by being.

That pine tree was my favorite tree companion, but other trees also played important roles in my life. The two central pines among the four were my kicking trees. Each spread out a branch toward the other in a way that approximated goal posts. Football stretched into winter, and my favorite team was the Green Bay Packers, a preference I shared with virtually every resident of my state. Paul Hornung was one of my favorite players, partly because of his Notre Dame background, but also because of his versatility. A top runner who also blocked, caught passes, occasionally threw one, and kicked, he scored points about every way it could be done on offense.

But it was his kicking that inspired my winter booting. And it was booting. Shod in my snow boots, bundled in a heavy coat, cap, and gloves, I carefully placed the football in a small clump of snow that served as the tee, and kicked my field goals right over the branches. Again and again, the snow flew as my foot swept upward, the old-fashioned, straight-ahead type of kicking no one does anymore.

The trees in the front yard also served me well in summer, during baseball season. I invented a lot of ways to play the game by myself, including the barn-wall baseball I described earlier. The elms along the eastern fence were the outfielders. I stood at the western fence, the large lilac bushes to my back, and tossed a rubber baseball into the air and swung my bat. If the ball missed the trees, I had a hit. If it soared above the elms, admittedly much shorter than the pines, I had a home run. But if the ball hit the branches, I was out, as surely as if Mickey Mantle had my ball firmly in his glove.

The drawback to the game was that I had to retrieve the ball, and sometimes I just did not feel like doing that. Fortunately, the four pines dropped an endless stream of pinecones. So with a smaller bat, I used the cones. In this baseball game, I faced the pines and tried to drive the cones through the trees without any branch intervening.

I recall my mother occasionally complaining that I was spreading the pinecones throughout the yard, especially when for a change of pace I would turn about ninety degrees and bash them against the elms. The cones made for unpleasant mowing. They would whiz right out from underneath the mower, the blades whipping them back off the mower's legs. Still, she never really interfered with any of my baseball versions, including the pinecone variety.

When I was in a more reflective mood, or I simply wanted to be alone and read, I would wander through the orchard west of our house, to a tall maple at the far end of the orchard. Its roots flayed out above the ground in order to make a comfortable, cradling seat. I would sit there and read, maybe think about Annette, whom I already mentioned, or write a little. I still remember reclining underneath that maple, wondering if the aforementioned rumor of her death was accurate, hoping it was not.

Someone else now owns the farm, and the maple is no longer there. I know some of the pines and elms remain, but the orchard does not. Unfortunately, my favorite tree, the climbing tree, unlike its fellow pines, and despite my affirmation of permanence in the poem above, died. Not long ago, the tree turned brown and eventually was cut down, leaving only a stump. Maybe the next time I have a chance to drive by the farm, I will take along my binoculars to see precisely which trees remain. On the other hand, it may be better not to know. One hates to learn that a good friend has gone away.

Dandelions

Most people consider dandelions weeds. They even attack them with various chemicals, destroying the dandelions along with assorted other weeds. Of course, technically, dandelions can play non-weed roles, occasionally providing salad greens or even wine. The general lot of the dandelion, though, is to be a weed, an enemy to an unblemished lawn.

We certainly had no aversion to chemicals on our farm, routinely applying fertilizers to our crops, especially corn. Poisoning weeds on the lawn, though, would have seemed an inappropriate, even wasteful, use of hard-earned money. Chemicals belonged totally to revenue-producing functions, although I doubt if my father ever in his whole life used the term *revenue*.

But to get to the really important point about dandelions requires leaving issues of chemicals and even weeds behind. Growing up, I never thought of a dandelion as anything other than a flower. And a flower that no one had to plant, water, and otherwise nurture. Thus it was the best of all types of flower, one freely given for our enjoyment.

Many times as a young boy I plucked dandelions for my mother. A bouquet of dandelions in a drinking glass, water up to the half or three-quarters mark, graced our kitchen table for many a meal. Looking back, I cannot remember or even imagine my mother asking, "What are you doing with those weeds in the house?" Or opining, "Somehow we should get rid of those weeds." Maybe, deep down, she would have preferred an uninterrupted rich green coating our lawn, but she never said so. She probably never even let such a thought trickle to the surface of her consciousness, lest she dishonor a special childhood gift that kept giving, all summer long, year after year.

Our children also brought us bouquets of dandelions. Just the other day one of our grandchildren brought us a bunch of dandelions clutched in her fist. When I look out and see scraggly weeds stretching above the grass, I know it's time to mow. But I never begrudge the bright yellow

Edward J. Rielly

dandelions their day. They bring back too many cherished memories of a time when beauty was all around us, ready to be plucked.

Professional Wrestling

I am almost ashamed to admit it, but I was enchanted with professional wrestling when I was a child. Television was in its own childhood then, and wrestling proved ideal for the medium. With the action confined to one reasonably small area, the competition was easy to film and easy to follow, even without instant replay.

So wrestling was one of the highlights of television programming in the 1950s, and it hooked me hard. I still remember a magazine I bought—a photo gallery of wrestling stars—and often wish I had held onto it. I traced the wrestlers onto white paper and cut them out. Then I constructed a wrestling ring on the bottom of a box turned upside down. I stuck a pencil in each corner for the posts and tied white string from post to post to complete the ring.

Then came the matches, the ring positioned on my bed, the outcome programmed, of course, by me. I naturally assumed that the wrestling I watched on television was on the up-and-up, but my "fixing" of my personal matches ironically paralleled the reality, especially as wrestling continued to develop over the next few decades.

So Pat O'Connor, Verne Gagne, Lou Thesz, Argentina Rocca, and Yukon Eric defeated the bad guys like Hans Schmidt, Buddy Rogers, and Killer Kowalski. O'Connor was my favorite, perhaps because of his Irish-sounding name and his good guy character. His skill was genuine, as he relied on technique and speed to overcome his (for wrestlers even then) modest size of some 220-230 pounds. By the time he became world heavyweight champion in 1959, my fascination with wrestling had waned, but I still followed my favorite's fortunes and was saddened when he lost to Buddy Rogers in the summer of 1961. I recall the match well. Each took one fall. Then O'Connor hurtled off the ropes to put a bruising block on Rogers. Unfortunately, the deceitful Rogers, always a villain, raised his knee and caught my champion in the head, knocking him cold and claiming the title.

Argentina Rocca was second to O'Connor in my favor. Rocca really was from Argentina, a former soccer player who had learned to use his feet as weapons. An acrobatic wrestler, Rocca liked to humiliate opponents (but only villains) by slapping them in the face with his bare feet. His favorite tactics included the drop kick, which he could deliver virtually from a standing position minus the running start other wrestlers required. I delighted to see him apply his pretzel hold to an adversary, crossing his ankles over the opponent's neck, securing his toes under it, and squeezing.

The coup de grace, though, was the backbreaker. He hoisted the victim onto his shoulders, right arm around one leg, left arm around the neck, and pulled. Victory came quickly.

I admired Verne Gagne for his clean-cut image, his college background (four times Big Ten wrestling champion at the University of Minnesota, along with two NCAA titles), and his real wrestling skill (he was selected as an alternate to the 1948 Olympic team). Yet I never entirely warmed to him, perhaps because he was just too quiet and reserved, too businesslike in how he went about his job. Lou Thesz, who seemed to go on forever, impressed me but also did not win my allegiance the way O'Connor and Rocca did.

Yukon Eric looked like a villain but wrestled like a good guy. For his time he was very big, weighing about 285 pounds, though that weight would not even make a good football lineman today. He was billed as hailing from the wilds of Canada, hence his name, but he actually was born in the state of Washington, which probably is close enough. And his real name was Eric Holmback. He wrestled barefoot, wearing blue jeans and a plaid wool shirt (the shirt always open and discarded before the match began).

Eric had suffered the indignity of losing part of an ear to a Killer Kowalski knee drop, but he got his revenge on many a villain, usually with a ferocious bear hug. He liked to grab the fellow by an arm and whip him against the ropes, catching him on the rebound against his massive chest, his treelike arms encircling and crushing. I never knew

Edward J. Rielly

until years later of his tragic end. One day in 1965, after he came home from tour and discovered that his wife had left home, taken all their money, and gone into hiding with their two children, Yukon Eric shot himself to death.

If I could have chosen death for a wrestler during my days as a fan, I would have picked Hans Schmidt. Born Guy Larose in Quebec, he likely was a good enough person in real life. But in the ring, he was the ultimate villain. With Nazi Germany still vivid in people's minds, Larose was billed as a German, Hans Schmidt, The Teuton Terror. He employed every dirty trick imaginable, hitting when he was ordered to break, kicking, choking. Then, while the hapless innocent gasped for breath, Hans would parade around the ring gesturing to the fans, exuding hatred and receiving plenty in return. He finished off his opponents with a backbreaker, though one different from Argentina Rocca's. Schmidt would hoist the softened-up adversary in his arms, kneel, and bring the wrestler down quickly, back first, on his knee. Never in the ring atop my bed did Hans Schmidt win. I meted out justice without fail. It was nice to be totally in control. Every hold came off just right, and every villain lost. Only when one good guy wrestled another did I have to consider the outcome. Of course, if Pat O'Connor was wrestling, the decision was easy.

Coming from a small town, I did not get to see my wrestling heroes live. However, one time my brother Joe, or Joey as I usually called him, took me to a wrestling match in the local high school gym. I did not know the wrestlers, who obviously were third- or fourth-tier competitors, but it was interesting to see a real ring up close. I may have felt a little disappointed in the quality, but at least I could say that I had been to a real wrestling match, even if the program did not include Pat O'Connor or Argentina Rocca.

A Lesson About Climbing

Two oats bins took up part of the top floor of our primary barn, the one in which we milked cows on the ground floor. We referred to the building as the white barn, as opposed to the red barn, which we used to store hay (also stored in the white barn), but which most importantly (for me) served as my baseball partner. Enough has been said about the red barn and baseball elsewhere in these reminiscences, although a word or two about my family's use of colors may be called for here.

Our color-coded references were quicker than identifying the barns by function, which inevitably would have required an additional phrase or two. "Where are you going?" "Out to the white barn." See how quick and easy that is? And it allows no room for error. Still, we also cared about the color as color. It was important that the white remained a fine bright white, and that the red retained its dark red cast. We saw to that through repeated paintings. Painting the white barn, though, which was much taller and generally larger in all its dimensions, was a huge task. We usually hired that done, with the painters using the process called whitewashing. That term has taken on a pejorative tone these days, referring to the covering up of dastardly deeds, but when I was growing up it just meant covering up dastardly boards that had faded out.

I have carried that fondness for color-coding through all these decades. "Which car are you taking?" my wife asks. "The green one," I say. She drives the red van. One might consider the word *van* sufficient, since we have only one, but that would be missing the point. The use of color carries a value all its own for me. It helps me tie present to past, which is good enough reason.

Back to the oats bins and climbing. A lattice arrangement of boards rose to the top of the first bin, an arrangement that facilitated climbing to the roof of the bin where hay bales were stored. The bin was an enclosed room right inside the large sliding doors that opened to permit a tractor and wagon to enter the barn. A passageway for the tractor was maintained between bins on the right and the haymow to the left. I was very young, maybe about five, when I decided that climbing to the top of the bin would be a good idea. And it was. I had no trouble navigating the interlocking boards that functioned as a ladder and soon reached the top. I explored the surface, covered by old hay dotted with pigeon droppings. We always referred to what pigeons did as "droppings," substituting direction for substance. After all, it always dropped, since pigeons invariably were above.

After perhaps ten or fifteen minutes, I tired of my explorations, or simply discovered all that was discoverable. The second bin I clearly recognized as impassible. It lacked the solid roof of the first one; only a few boards stretched across its top. So when I finished exploring the first oats bin, I was unable to cross onto the next one and decided that it was time to descend. Then came the problem.

The means of descent was the same as for ascent, but I now had to back down, placing a foot where I could not see its destination, no matter how hard I tried to twist my neck around. Fear overtook me, and I alternated calling for help and just sitting there on the roof of the oats bin waiting.

Finally, my brother Joey heard me and came to my rescue. He climbed up and persuaded me to follow him down, which I did, one of his hands steadying me, guiding my searching shoe while he held on to the ladder with his other hand. So we descended what was probably about eight feet. I could have jumped, landed in a soft, cushioning layer of hay, and probably been no worse for the landing, but that had also seemed too frightening. Eight feet can be a long way for a five-year-old.

I learned a lesson about climbing through this experience: not to attempt a climb unless you are sure that you can get back down again. Certainly I did not attempt that climb again until I was a bit older. However, that failed effort at climbing back down helped teach me an even more important lesson: one about brothers. It helped me recognize better what brothers are for: to help each other. That final lesson came to me more vividly years later when I no longer had any brothers left. I wrote a poem about this childhood experience from this much wiser perspective:

Hands Reaching

A young boy, I was primed
for climbing, eyeing the oats bin
and its top, a crosshatching of boards
flaked with end-of-year fragments
left over from the top's
double duty as a hayloft.

I climbed and climbed, up the wooden
ladder, foot reaching gingerly for
the next step, hands gripping and
pulling, even a young boy's weight heavy.
I made it and exulted, exulted

all too soon. There came a time
when getting down was even more vital
than climbing up. But that distance
multiplied looking down, and neither hands
nor feet could move me down that crawl.

So I called, and my brother answered,
years older, years taller, strong
shoulders and long arms stretching,
reaching my straining hands, my hands
in his, the rest of me coming naturally.

Years later my brother, in his quiet, dark
living room reached and fell,
his large, much older body tumbling
to the floor, silent on a carpet brown as hay,
leaving me nights I dream about long
arms reaching for a frightened boy.

Edward J. Rielly

My Roy Rogers Rifle and Other Toys

Toys can take on added importance for a child who does not have other children nearby to play with. Such was my condition. I had a lot of toys for the times. Some might say that was because I was the youngest and the youngest tend to get some favored treatment. If that were the case, so be it! I loved my toys.

Of course, they were not like toys today. Not much in the way of electrical or battery-operated gizmos. If I wanted my toys to move, I had to move them. They did not talk to me, and they never, ever operated through the screen of our black-and-white television. Computers were far in the future, not even something that I could imagine. To put it bluntly, toys were simpler.

Over the years, most of my toys eventually broke, a great many while they were stored in the "Far Room" of our house. Other objects got placed on top of them, and increasingly brittle plastic cracked, old tin bent, glue dissolved, and paper went the way of all paper (and flesh).

Ready to go after a bear in my Davy Crockett shirt and coonskin cap.

Model plastic airplanes and ships finally fell off their pedestals, wings drooped, and hulls came apart.

When my mother died many years after I had grown up and had children of my own, we had to clear out that storage room prior to selling the farm. A lot of toys went into the trash because they were too broken to keep. But the best of the lot, some of my favorites that I had stored with extra care, and some others that had endured better than others, survived to make the long trek from Wisconsin to Maine. They now occupy shelves in a small storage room in my house. My grandchildren like them, and under their grandfather's very watchful eyes they are permitted from time to time to play with them.

I grew up long before the debate over whether children should be given toy guns. I had a veritable arsenal. Some remain, including my prized plastic Roy Rogers rifle. His signature is right there on the stock, and most of the gold coloring is still present. The trigger still clicks, the hammer continues to cooperate, the barrel points as true as ever. I can bring down a gang of outlaws as easily now as when I was a youngster keeping our farm free of rustlers and bandits. The rifle was a special favorite of my grandson. He became as skilled a shot as I, but we kept that from his parents. Unfortunately, unlike me, he seems to have outgrown the rifle.

My Davy Crockett cap no longer fits but otherwise is little the worse for wear. Yes, the image of Davy Crockett on the fake leather on the top of the hat is faded a bit, but the fake raccoon hair is still as soft and smooth, and the tail, still attached, dangles as heroically as ever. My Hubley flintlock still fires both barrels, though I have none of those little paper caps to place under the hammers anymore, and I have to be careful of the handle, where the plastic is cracked.

The Old West (or some fictional version of it) was dear to my heart during childhood. In addition to the guns, I had a cowboy outfit complete with hat, chaps, and gun belt, as well as a wealth of small plastic cowboys, Indians, and horses. They fought many a battle around our yard, alternating their wars with those fought by my multitude of toy soldiers (World War II variety). But perhaps the finest cowboy toy I owned, and which retains its pristine condition today—a sure sign of the value I placed on it—is a Roy Rogers stagecoach that my sister brought back for me from a trip she took, to Chicago, I think. Although plastic, it evinces not a crack or chip. The wheels twirl perfectly, the two side doors open effortlessly, and the small rifle rides yet in its holder beside the driver. The driver, a miniature Roy Rogers, retains his removable whip, and his horses prance as nimbly as ever, their harnesses impeccable. Let anyone who thinks he owns a finer Roy Rogers stagecoach dare put his up against mine.

Farm toys also were among my favorites, an assertion that may strike some people as odd, since the real things surrounded me every day. Yet there I was with my toy versions. Most have passed into oblivion, but a few remain, especially the farm implements. Heading the list is my toy Allis-Chalmers tractor. My father was a loyal Wisconsinite, owning two of the tractors built at West Allis, Wisconsin: a WC and a WD. Both, like all Allis-Chalmers tractors, were bright orange (technically Persian Orange), but the paint faded out during the many years we owned them. Tractors, like men's suits, tended to last for almost the life span of the farmer.

The WC model was introduced in the 1930s and was a historically important tractor; it was the first Allis-Chalmers built for pneumatic tires (as opposed to tires with steel rims). The WD was newer, coming out shortly after World War II. My toy tractor is a WD. Regrettably, the Allis-Chalmers tractor is now only a part of our national history rather than of our national present. The company was eaten up by a German company that was eventually swallowed by an even bigger fish, becoming the Allis-Gleaner Company. In December 1985, the last Allis-Chalmers tractors slinked out of the West Allis plant, making for a sad Christmas.

Other implements, of course, were also essential on my play farm. Those that remain include a splendid Oliver hay baler and, from the same company, a combine, which replaced the threshing machine. Then, to ensure that the roads remained level in the summer and cleared of snow in the fall, I owned a road grader. It remains one of my most prized toys. Like the stagecoach, the road grader is in tiptop shape. All the tires are well inflated, the front set still turns at the command of the steering wheel, and the blade may be used at various angles, the better to remove imaginary snow or smooth imaginary gravel on one's imaginary road. Like all road graders that called themselves real road graders in those days, it is yellow.

Perhaps there is something metaphorically appropriate about the toy animals that have survived. Most farm creatures have gone to their eternal toy reward, but the ferocious animals, those that would just as soon eat you or toss you over a hilltop, remain: the lion, the rhinoceros, the hippopotamus, the elephant. And they are just as intimidating as when I was a child. At night, I am especially careful upon entering the little room where they abide.

Hamburgers and Fries
Under the Golden Arches

McDonald's is everywhere today, not only in the United States, but also throughout the world. When I was growing up, it was not so. We did not visit McDonald's much. In fact, we seldom ate out, so eating anywhere other than home was a treat, even if my mother's meals were regularly delicious.

It was especially exciting for me when, on rare occasions, I got to eat at McDonald's. There were no franchises nearby then, the closest being in Madison. Occasionally we went to the state's capital city, usually my sister driving as she was older than I and therefore had her driver's license long before I received mine. We visited shops, and even back then bookstores were my favorite. I am definitely a bookstore junkie, able to wander for hours through a bookstore and then return again the next evening. Some people when bored go to the local bar for a drink. I go to a bookstore to look at books.

Well, back to McDonald's. Today I cannot explain satisfactorily why the fast-food chain was such a thrill. Certainly it was a different experience for me, and the food was different. The hamburgers were small, but they were still hamburgers, and I did not get hamburgers at home. Steaks, pork chops, ribs, liver, chicken, turkey, but not hamburgers.

Edward J. Rielly

Nor did I get French fries at home, although we had potatoes virtually every day, usually boiled potatoes, an Irish specialty that I still love. But French fries, like hamburgers, were restaurant foods, and we did not often go to restaurants. Maybe if I had grown up in a city, I would have had my fill of hamburgers early on.

McDonald's had started as a small-time business in California in 1940 and began to spread as Ray Kroc started opening franchises in 1955. The real boom in McDonald's did not occur until Kroc bought out the MacDonald brothers (the name really had that extra "a" in it) in 1961. By 1965, Kroc was operating some seven hundred McDonald's hamburger places throughout the country and contributing mightily to the fattening of America.

However, nobody worried about calories and saturated fat when I was growing up. Grease was a good thing, adding real taste to food. Most mothers, as far I could tell, kept a cup or some other container full of bacon drippings on the kitchen stove, saved from frying bacon, to use later when frying other food. My wife tells of dipping bread in the bacon drippings when she was a child, a practice certain to make modern dieticians throw up their hands in horror. When my mother ran out of bacon drippings, she had to resort to lard. She bought the lard in large containers. We went through it fast.

So the fatty food from McDonald's was great. On those rare trips to the big city, we would buy several hamburgers or cheeseburgers each. There were no Big Macs yet, I believe. And we devoured fries sprinkled with tons of salt. The price was right, too. As I recall, a hamburger cost about fifteen cents, which I think was the same as a pack of French fries. A cheeseburger was a few cents more. I considered it money well spent. When I drive past a McDonald's today, I can feel my arteries clogging just from the memory of those burgers and fries.

The Steel Helmet

The first movie that most children see is usually a kid-friendly animated film. In my day, that likely would have been a Walt Disney film, maybe featuring Cinderella or Snow White or Bambi. The first big movie experience for my son was *Star Wars*, although that was not his first excursion to a movie house. There is a difference, of course, between one's first film and the first film that one really remembers seeing. This distinction is a prelude to my earliest recollection of a film.

I may have seen others before, but the earliest movie I can remember seeing, strangely enough, was not a cute Disney feature but a Korean War production: *The Steel Helmet*. The movie came out in 1951, when I was about eight years old. I remember it well.

We saw it in the theater in Mineral Point, Wisconsin, an old operahouse-type structure that has been remodeled in recent years and still, to the best of my knowledge, offers movies. It also is available for concerts and other events. Recently, I went back to Mineral Point for a literary festival, much of which occurred in the same old theater where I had seen that war film.

Looking back, I kind of wonder about my being taken to the movie. *The Steel Helmet* is not particularly appropriate for young children. A Sergeant Zack, a World War II veteran played by Gene Evans, who spent a big chunk of his career playing in Westerns, is the protagonist. Zack is the lone survivor of an American infantry unit that is captured by the North Koreans, who then execute all of the prisoners except him. What saves Zack is his steel helmet of the title, which deflects the would-be executioner's bullet.

Zack's hands are untied by a Korean orphan (William Chun), and the two set off to find friends. They pick up a medic and then run into an American patrol led by a green Lieutenant Driscoll, played by Steve Brodie. Zack saves the patrol when snipers pin it down. The film gets pretty heavy at times, even beyond the fighting. U.S. racial issues come out, and a prisoner, a North Korean major (Harold Fong), is deliberately

Edward J. Rielly

killed by an angry Zack. Driscoll later asks Zack to exchange helmets for luck, but the veteran sergeant refuses, and Driscoll is subsequently killed during a successful repelling of an enemy attack. At the conclusion of the film, Zack pauses at Driscoll's grave, which is marked with his helmet, and makes the exchange, finally doing what the lieutenant had requested.

Samuel Fuller was the force behind the film, writing and directing it as well as serving as co-producer. He made it on a shoestring, rushing through filming in ten days and filming in a studio and a park. The cost was just over $100,000, but the film earned some $6 million. The Army did not like it, especially the depiction of a soldier killing a prisoner; but Fuller, a real World War II veteran, defended the movie's realism and even called on his former commander, Brigadier General George Taylor, to confirm that killing prisoners did sometimes occur.

The film is worth seeing and clearly offers an effective lesson on how to choose a really good title that truly represents the content of a film, but I still cannot quite figure out how I managed to get into that movie. Maybe if I could remember for sure who took me, the answer would be clearer. I suspect that it may have been one of my older brothers, or maybe both of them. It definitely is a movie they would have liked, and, being brothers, they probably would have been a little more lenient than my parents about what I saw.

The effect of *The Steel Helmet* on me obviously was sufficient for me to remember it. I do not recall being frightened by it or absorbing the significance of the racial content. The action, however, was far more violent than anything I would have seen before. I think that the combat and the death of Driscoll were what especially affected me. War films have long been one of my favorite film genres. I cannot, of course, prove a cause-to-effect relationship between that early war film and this preference, although *The Steel Helmet* clearly did not prevent my enjoying many other war movies.

Pink Gum by the Ton

Elsewhere I have noted my fascination with baseball cards and my massive collecting of them, and the games I played with my baseball cards, much to the detriment of my potential retirement funds. Yet there was something else about my baseball card collecting that remains firmly in my memory if no longer in my mouth: pink gum.

I came upon a pink stain on one of my baseball cards the other day and felt as if I were right back in my childhood. Of course, collectors look unfavorably on such stains, putting the defacement right up there with all of the other imperfections that devalue an otherwise fiscally valuable card, such as pen or pencil markings and rounded corners.

So what about this gum? Well, each pack of cards came with a thin rectangular slab of pink gum, covered in a fine pink layer of gum dust. Truth be told, it did not taste all that good, but nonetheless I chewed it, blew bubbles with it. Waste not, want not.

Sometimes, though, a package of baseball cards might sit in the car, sun beating down, as I perhaps accompanied my mother into a store. Warm sunshine did not help the gum; in fact, it tended to melt the gum into the closest card, leaving a pink stain that could not be removed with any technology known then, or invented since. A pink gum stain is forever.

I could pry the gum off the card, and, for my purposes, the card still sufficed. If the gum had collected a bit of cardboard or ink, I might toss the gum away—might—but not likely. As I said, waste not, want not. That proverb first appeared in the eighteenth century according to my *Oxford Dictionary of Quotations*, not, of course, about baseball cards and gum, but it still applies.

That pink gum has vanished from packages of baseball cards, I am told. The gum became undesirable once collecting baseball cards turned mercenary. Collectors had learned to preserve the financial value of the cards. And if purchasers of baseball cards wanted gum, they could find far tastier types than those pink slabs. Yet I would not mind a chew once again. Any old pink gum lying around out there?

Edward J. Rielly

Boy and Other Dogs

In my rural community, a farm without a dog was almost unheard of. Some dogs assisted with the work a bit, helping to bring the milk cows up to the barn from a back pasture, for example. My dogs, however, were primarily pets, companions, to be more precise.

As the youngest child in my family, and given that the other farms were far enough away to require a good walk to get to them, I spent a lot of my spare time by myself. That is where my dogs came in. It's not that I actually played with them a lot; they were just there with me, a comfort when I felt down, keeping me company when I felt alone—or was alone. That meant a lot.

Boy, my first dog, and I share a stare, just in different directions.

I had one dog at a time. My dad would make the arrangements, but he certainly did not go to a pet store to buy a dog. There were plenty of farm families with dogs having puppies.

Naming was not exclusively my role, but I had a lot of input. I hesitate to admit that my choices came up short on imagination, but they did express my perception of our dogs as more than mere animals. I chose generic gender-specific terms: Boy, Lady, Lassie (the latter borrowed from the popular television show of the time). My naming actually followed the family tradition. Before I came along, my family had a dog named Laddie.

Boy was my first dog. He was black and white and part Collie. What else he may have been I never knew. Boy was fond of the whole family but especially felt a responsibility to me. One day when I was very young—during my preschool years—I wandered close to the fence separating our front yard from the gravel road that ran by our farm. In truth, I was in no danger because I could not get through the fence by myself, but Boy was not aware of that. He heard a truck coming, saw me near the road, and went into action. Boy raced across the lawn, grabbed me by the collar of my shirt, and started pulling. He was determined to keep me from being run over by that truck.

It was not a truck that eventually caused Boy's death, but a neighbor. Boy often followed my dad out to the fields. On one particular day, he followed him to a field adjacent to this neighbor's farm. Dad returned, but Boy stayed behind, perhaps to chase a rabbit, or just to sniff out the area a bit more.

When Boy never returned, Dad went looking for him. The exact time frame escapes me now, but it probably was the following day, maybe even later, when Dad found out what had happened. Unable to locate my dog, Dad stopped in to ask the neighbors if they had seen Boy. This neighbor, at that point, admitted that he had shot Boy, claiming that he was chasing his sheep. We never believed him because that was not something Boy had ever done. Besides, the neighbor certainly knew whose dog it was and could easily have mentioned the problem to my dad if, in fact, there were a problem.

Why he shot Boy remains a mystery. Maybe just meanness. I never forgave him for that. I can forgive a lot, but killing my dog without cause was just too much.

Lassie, like her TV counterpart, was a traditional-looking Collie. Her temperament was placid, and she was a fine dog. I never felt quite as close to her as to Lady, though. Lady, a combination Collie and Shepherd, doubled as my babysitter. When the rest of the family went somewhere without me—which did not occur often—I would invite Lady into the house with me. Our dogs, like most farm dogs, were not housedogs. Even in bad winter weather, they seldom came into the house, although a doghouse or the barn would offer refuge from ice and snow. However, I would welcome Lady into the kitchen, where she would make herself comfortable on our old Morris chair. A guest needs a little treat, so I would bring out something to drink. Root beer pleased her, and we would have a drink while passing the time.

Edward J. Rielly

Lady's death, which was from natural causes, bothered me a lot, probably because I watched her slowly die. My parents pronounced her dead, but I remained unconvinced—denial we would call it now. I recall asking if they were sure, and, if somehow they were mistaken, whether she could claw her way up through the dirt that we placed over her. The question sounds pretty silly now, but the affirmative answer to that second question gave me some comfort—just in case. We buried her outside the yard fence between two trees not far from where my dad usually parked our truck. It was a nice spot, one that I passed regularly.

Years later I wrote a poem based on Lady's death. I did what writers sometimes do when writing about an especially sad moment. I established some distance between the event and myself, in this case by changing a few of the facts, including making the dog male. It is entitled "A Way of Ending":

> The dog died quietly, sensing perhaps
> that the pain would pass like a dewclaw
> cut too close, or a splinter slowly
> working its way out—how before he
> had slept pain away, his body drawn
> into a circle in a corner of our kitchen.
>
> He couldn't grasp the distinction, not even
> when the light went out in midday
> and the rumble in his throat gradually
> receded like an echo in a long, dark cave.
> He just lay his golden head down as if
> for sleep, breathed slowly, and then breathed
> not at all.

Church Mission

Going to church may not seem like a lot of fun for most children, but there was one special church event that I enjoyed a lot. That was the annual mission at Holy Rosary Catholic Church in Darlington. The mission involved several evenings and was conducted by a visiting priest. I must admit that I remember almost nothing about the actual evening services, although they included, as one would expect, a lot of praying and sermons.

What I liked about the mission was the sort of store that was set up in the entryway to the church. After the service, we could look the items over and buy whatever we needed or wanted. The items included statues, prayer books, rosaries, candles, holy pictures, holy water containers, and other things associated with how we lived our faith.

Maybe I was just a really odd kid, but I loved looking at all of this. The statues especially appealed to me. In fact, my parents, acceding to my requests, bought me two statues during these annual missions: one of Jesus and one of the Virgin Mary. I still have them. I'll start with Jesus.

To be honest, the Jesus statue is not much. Now, I know that Jesus is more important than Mary, but his statue is not very impressive, objectively speaking. Of course, it was quite important to me at the time—still is, but aesthetically it remains a bit deficient. The statue stands about eight inches tall and is plastic. The pose is a common one, with Jesus holding his left hand to his red heart, which appears on the outside of his chest. The right hand is raised in a blessing. He wears a red robe with a golden trim, certainly a finer robe than Jesus ever wore during his life. The statue, which I kept on a shelf in my bedroom, helped make Jesus more real to me. I was praying to someone whose image I could see. It remains important to me as a reminder of my youthful faith.

The Mary statue is made of plaster and rises to thirteen inches above the base. Her bare feet hold down a snarling serpent. Her arms hang at her sides, palms forward as if they were welcoming a young boy who was much taken with the Mary image. Her blue robe, as with the Jesus statue, certainly is richer than what the actual woman wore. She still looks young in this statue, not the middle-aged mother of the adult Jesus. Her posture is simple and direct—even passive, one might say, as little effort seems required of her to hold the evil serpent in check. Despite the apparent passivity, there is a kind of life to the statue, especially in Mary's face. Her eyes are downcast, looking casually (rather

Edward J. Rielly

than staring) at the serpent. Her nose is somewhat long and sharp, and a tinge of red colors her lips. Her long brown hair hangs to her shoulders, escaping her veil. She looks like a real person.

I also had a large picture of the Virgin Mary hanging in my bedroom. She was very young in that picture, even younger than she appears in the statue. Mary was a comforting presence, and her roles were quite substantial in my young life. I was told—and, of course, completely believed—that she was the intercessor. If I really wanted something, it was better to ask Mary to ask Jesus rather than to go directly to Jesus. Who, after all, can turn down a mother's request? Not even God would do that! I still find myself at times praying that way.

She was also the person I was told to keep in mind for that future moment when I would be dying—not, of course, a particularly happy thought for a child. At that moment, she was the one to whom I should pray. The "Hail Mary" prayer clearly enunciated that final role for Mary in my life: "Pray for us sinners now and at the hour of our death, Amen." Wow! It was good to have someone ready to take over at that crucial moment, especially someone whose son—which is to say God—could not ignore. Me he could perhaps damn to perdition, but not if his mother were there paving the way for me.

So I was permitted to become the owner of those two statues. I went home happy from our parish missions, content and secure in my youthful certitude that Jesus and Mary were not only God and his mother, but also my friends.

Confession

Being Irish-Catholic meant that I grew up in an attitudinal mix that fused a Catholic emphasis on sin with Irish guilt. The locus of that sin and guilt, of course, was the Ten Commandments. Each evening before going to sleep, a good Catholic boy was encouraged to engage in an examination of conscience to determine the day's violations of one or more of the Commandments, the point being, I think, that I would have the opportunity to repent of my sins in case I died during the night, thus giving me a fighting chance to at least make it to Purgatory. I usually bypassed this evening ritual and took my chances.

What I could not bypass, however, was going to confession. The technical name of this experience was Penance, one of the seven sacraments, the one especially connected to the Ten Commandments because I was expected to admit during confession my violations of the commandments.

My family regularly went to confession. Saturday afternoon was the usual time, although our priests also heard confessions (the colloquial term for the priest's role) before Sunday Masses.

For those who are unfamiliar with what confession was like then, I should describe the process. It has changed a lot, and not necessarily for the better from a child's perspective. Would you rather confess your sins anonymously in a dark room as we did then or face to face with the priest? We did the former. That anonymity, however, had its limitations.

Penance was a popular sacrament during my childhood, unlike today when it has largely disappeared from the lives of most Catholics. When we arrived on Saturday, a lot of other people would also be in the church. Preparation was the first step. No matter how ready one might be upon arriving—remember those evening examinations of conscience?—one had to demonstrate readiness by kneeling for a time in a pew and meditating on one's sins. Forgetting any sins was not good.

So after a period spent in remembering and (perhaps) praying, it was time to take one's place in the line of penitents standing alongside (sometimes leaning against, but only children would do anything so disrespectful) a wall. Because we had two confessionals and two priests hearing confessions, we had two lines of penitents. One line by one wall went to one confessional, the other to the other. Sometimes one line would be a lot longer than the other, depending on which priest occupied a particular confessional. Children especially liked to strategize confession, opting for the more lenient and understanding priest (translated, the younger priest), and above all avoiding a priest who spoke loudly. "You had how many impure thoughts?" Such a question radiating from the confessional would make any youngster long to turn invisible so that he could escape the confessional unseen and unrecognized.

Now for the confessional: imagine a tall closet-like room partitioned into three parts. Each section had its own entrance. The priest occupied the central section, which actually had a door. A dark curtain hung over the entrance to each of the other little rooms. The priest sat on a chair or stool with a window leading into each of the other cubicles. The window had a sliding wooden shutter that could be slid open. A net of some sort remained, seriously impeding vision, so that one could see only a dark outline through it. Theoretically, the sinner was to remain anonymous, but, of course, a priest who knew his parishioners well would certainly be able to identify many of the penitents. That thought was especially troubling for children, even with the Seal of Confession firmly planted on the priest's lips. We all understood that the priest was obliged to die rather than divulge anything he heard in the confessional. Still, one could worry a bit. If nothing else, would he remember your sins the next time he saw you? "Ah, there's the boy with all those impure thoughts." Or, "There's the boy who disobeys his parents."

People tended to remain fairly far away from the confessional, deliberately trying not to overhear anything emanating from it. Sometimes, though, a murmur might escape, occasionally even a statement. Most to be feared—and avoided at all costs—was the hard-of-hearing priest, as a child would rather die than have to shout out his transgressions.

There also were telltale warnings for those children not completely familiar with the priests. After all, not every family went to confession as often as mine. The most obvious warning was a major discrepancy in the length of lines. A short line was to be avoided like the plague. It might save time, but for a child that short line meant danger, loud and clear. Those folks in the long line knew something important, and a child had better take notice. Perhaps that short-line priest spoke too loudly, gave heavy penances, or chastised severely.

Once inside the confessional, I waited while the priest finished with the person on the other side. Then the little shutter slid, and the priest's face appeared through the netting. "Bless me, Father, for I have sinned," I would begin, and then convey how long ago my last confession was and relate my transgressions, both type (in as general terms as I could get away with) and number. The number could be tough to estimate, but I figured that God would accept a best guess.

If all went well, the priest would abstain from commentary and merely give me my penance, typically a certain number of "Our Father's" and "Hail Mary's." The window would close, and I would brush aside the curtain and return to the pew. Technically, one did not have to say one's penance immediately, but it was always good to get it over with. Forgetting, after all, would wipe out the whole effect of the confession. Naturally, one would not want to spend too much time praying in the pew for fear that observers might conclude a serious level of sin. Similarly, spending a lot of time in the confessional also boded ill. There were so many complexities and nuances involved in this confession process.

So there you have it. That was what I underwent again and again during my childhood. I could do it today in my sleep. As a matter of fact, given the choice, I would rather do it in my sleep.

The Rosary

One of our family religious rituals was the evening Rosary. The Rosary consists of a sequence of prayers usually grouped in five sets, each set (or "decade") consisting of one "Our Father" and ten "Hail Mary's." There are some other dimensions to it as well, including introductory prayers and a special name for each decade of prayers depending on the day of the week. All of this required a certain amount of memorizing, although the basic prayers were so common that we all knew them inside and out.

As we prayed, we knelt facing and leaning on a chair. The Rosary required about fifteen minutes, and kneeling straight up without support that long would have bordered on torture.

"Saying" the Rosary (the common term for praying it), may not seem like something a young boy would necessarily enjoy, but I enjoyed it. I may not have cared a great deal for our usual praying of the Rosary;

Edward J. Rielly

in fact, knowing the "Our Father" and "Hail Mary" so well invited an almost unconscious recitation with the words slurring together and speedily sliding through.

However, occasionally my father, who usually led us in the Rosary, allowed me to lead. The leader would say the opening segment of a prayer and the others would recite the remainder. That I very much enjoyed. In fact, it was a special thrill for me to lead the evening prayer. Perhaps it was more the chance to be the leader—a sort of performance—than exalted holiness.

I have no recollection of anyone other than Dad or me leading the Rosary. Maybe it was viewed as a male activity, or maybe I was so self-focused that I simply cannot remember others doing it. In any case, leading the Rosary was a special treat and a not insignificant part of my childhood—but it is one of those parts I have largely left behind. Like other important moments of childhood, though, I relive it in my memory if not in practice.

Traded For a Pig

Now, I want to make it absolutely clear that I felt very loved by my parents—most of the time. However, there were moments when I might not have been absolutely confident about that love: whenever we visited a small grocery store—what folks in some parts of the country today might call a variety store—in Waldwick, Wisconsin. The proprietor, Matt Ross, was a jovial man who liked to crack a joke. A young child, though, sometimes has a hard time distinguishing between a joke and a serious statement. Such was the case with an offer that Mr. Ross raised from time to time when my parents arrived with me in tow to do some shopping. The offer: a pig in exchange for me.

My parents, fortunately, never accepted the offer, and the extent to which they considered it remains a bit unclear. At least it was unclear to me then. My father would listen to the offer, seem to mull it over for a time, hem and haw a bit, and then decline the deal. Yet Dad's rejection never seemed absolute, for the offer would raise its troubling head again on our next visit to the store.

I enjoyed visiting the store, as it featured a little of everything, including candy. Still, I was always somewhat uneasy about that trade offer.

Looking back, I imagine that my parents did not sound definitive about rejecting it because they were just playing along. At least I hope so. In any case, I like to think that my parents made the right decision in turning it down.

Swing and a Hammock

Life was busy on the farm. During the summer, there was work to do from sunup until long after sundown. Nevertheless, moments for rest and relaxation did come along, and two means to that end were our swing and our hammock.

The swing was primarily for kids, although I recall a priceless picture of my father dressed, as usual, in his overalls, swinging on the swing. Or maybe he was just sitting on it. I assume that the picture was posed because I cannot remember my dad ever actually swinging.

Mary and I taking a swing for two under the old swing tree.

I did swing, though, and so did my siblings when they were young. The seat was sawed out of a wooden board with a notch at each end that the rope went through. The rope stretched underneath the seat and up toward a tree branch. The two ends of the rope were tied securely around the branch.

Edward J. Rielly

The seat was not the most secure in the world, resting, as it did, on a thick rope, although the end notches helped to keep the seat in place. However, I recall no serious accidents. I would swing out toward the house, over the dirt underneath, the ground worn bare from so many push-offs from feet, the initial means of acceleration.

Then, grasping the two vertical portions of the rope, I would continue to accelerate, using a well coordinated up and forward motion of my body while propelling my legs back and then suddenly forward. It was great fun, although not exactly restful.

The hammock, however, was just the ticket for resting. It was orange with several inches of fringe on its sides and a permanently attached pillow. The hammock was connected at the head to a large, thick tree, and at the foot to a square wooden post. Several hooks in the tree and post permitted the hammock to be raised or lowered to coincide with the age or daring of the person lying in it. Of course, two could sit side by side and use it as a sort of swing as well.

When a breeze was blowing, the rustling leaves in the tree made a great fan, and one could doze off in the hammock with little to bother him or her except for an occasional pesky bug.

For all the times that I sat, swung, or reclined in the hammock, I have never owned one since. I could, of course, buy a hammock that comes with a freestanding frame, but a hammock not connected to a tree has never seemed like the real deal to me. I don't give up, however, on someday having a tree that will be just right for an old-fashioned hammock, preferably one made from soft orange cloth with a lot of fringe.

Rheumatic Fever

I developed rheumatic fever just as I was heading into my teen years. My mother often referred then and in later years to listening to my heart and hearing the sound of crackling. The illness included a leaking heart valve, which means that the valve did not close completely, allowing some blood to seep back into the portion of the heart from which the blood was flowing. That might have been what she was hearing. I have no idea whether her description was accurate. It sounds awful, and regardless of what strange sounds may or may not have emanated from my heart, it was an unpleasant time, one from which I fortunately recovered entirely.

Everyone in my family took the illness quite seriously, although they tried not to worry me. I do not recall being frightened of the diagnosis; it just was a period in my life, which probably demonstrates more than anything—except my recovery—what an effective job my family did in handling my illness, especially in keeping me from worrying a lot.

I spent several weeks in bed, but in our parlor rather than upstairs. That way I remained more involved in the daily life of our family and seemed much less ill than if I had been packed away in my usual bedroom.

I spent a lot of time reading during those weeks. I read "real" books, of course, but also comic books. A schoolmate, Dale Hess, came up to visit periodically and brought comics as well. I did not have many visits from schoolmates, partly because there were not many children in my school (usually about thirteen in all); and since they were all farm children with chores to do, they did not have a lot of time to come calling. Sadly, Dale died suddenly of a heart attack when he was still in high school.

Another visitor was Monsignor Bernard Doyle, our pastor at Holy Rosary Catholic Church in Darlington. Father Doyle took his pastoral duties seriously, and caring for the families in his parish was part of his responsibilities, a part that he seemed to care a great deal about. My family had been members of the parish for a long time, and Father Doyle, who could be stern when sternness was called for, did not neglect his flock. Ireland born, Father Doyle perhaps had a special soft spot in his heart for Irish families.

In any case, this was not the first major interaction that my family had with Father Doyle. When my brother, Lawrence, drowned in 1955, Father Doyle arrived at the river where divers were searching for my brother. He stayed there during the search, providing considerable comfort to my parents and family.

Edward J. Rielly

Then in December of 1956, again prior to my bout with rheumatic fever, my sister, Mary, became terribly ill with hepatitis. For some time, the doctors in Darlington were unable to diagnose Mary's illness, and she became so ill that Father Doyle gave her the last rites of the Church, something in those days administered only to people who were in serious danger of dying. Today the sacrament is more commonly referred to as the anointing of the sick, with the anointing administered to those who are likely to recover as well as to those who are near death. The sacrament is intended to help effect both spiritual and physical healing. Father Doyle, though, was not ready to give up on Mary's recovery. He became irate at the doctors for not doing more to cure Mary and offered to put her in his own car and drive her to a Madison hospital. Fortunately, a Dr. Witte from Monroe, Wisconsin, who was called in to consult, diagnosed the hepatitis and set Mary on the path to recovery.

It was a very worrisome Christmas season that year. My brother Joey took me to Christmas Mass at night, and I was so tired that I struggled to stay awake. All turned out well, though, and Mary came through this ordeal so that she could resume her teaching and continue to be the best sister one could ever have. I might add that Christmas of 1956 was when I received an electric train as a gift—a huge gift at the time given its expense. The train was a gift from Mary, bought with money from her first teaching job, at Johnson School a few miles south of our farm.

My staying at home with rheumatic fever was interrupted by regular trips into Darlington to see our doctor. The blood tests were the worst part of those trips, setting me on a path to despise all sorts of needles ever since. However, recovery was relatively swift, and eventually I resumed my school days at Fort Defiance and a full range of activities, including those barn baseball games recounted elsewhere in this book.

Comic Books

I bought lots of comic books in the 1950s, even into the early 1960s, and enjoyed them immensely. Comic books were not expensive in those days, a typical book going for a dime, and a fat, omnibus-type comic book for a quarter. I could walk into a variety store or drugstore with a fifty-cent piece and leave with five comics, good for several hours of reading and mulling over the fate of my favorite characters.

The period of my youth was very different from today, a much more innocent time in many ways. Superheroes are all the rage as we move deeper into the twenty-first century, but few made my set of favorite characters. Superman was the exception. I occasionally bought comic books featuring the man who leaps tall buildings and outraces a speeding bullet. But he was a reasonably innocent figure as well, always catching the villains without killing them, as good consistently triumphed over evil; in fact, his other self, Clark Kent, came across as innocent and just a little bamboozled by life. When he dashed into a phone booth or closet to change, emerging as the world's champion, he did his crime fighting right: minimal violence and consistent humility.

Mainly, though, I liked cartoon characters. There were Looney Tunes comics featuring the stable of Looney Tunes figures: Bugs Bunny and Porky Pig, both often confused, irresponsible, and endlessly in trouble, were not unlike kids. Sylvester the cat was eternally in conflict with little Tweety Bird and harbored a consistently unfulfilled desire to have his tiny adversary for lunch. Always, however, Tweety outwitted Sylvester, who, in the final analysis, was really not so bad after all. Elmer Fudd, with his speech defect, and Daffy Duck, who was, well, daffy, also were consistently in conflict.

Other comic books featured not a medley of Looney Tunes characters but primarily one: Bugs Bunny and Porky Pig, especially. And, of course, there were the quarter comics, providing even more hours of fun. Often they were built around a theme, e.g., *Bugs Bunny's Halloween Fun Trick 'N' Treat*. The Looney Tunes folks could get really clever with special issues. In *Bugs Bunny's Album*, for example, Bugs shows us photographs and narrates the stories of famous Bunny ancestors, including Alexander Graham Bunny, inventor of the portable hole; Bushy Bunny, a great musician in the time of Nero; and Ali Baba Bunny, who discovered the secret of the Forty Thieves. All of those ancestors, strangely enough, looked and acted a whole lot like Bugs.

Edward J. Rielly

Yet even more than the Looney Tunes characters, I enjoyed Walt Disney creations. I spent many hours with Donald Duck and his rather dysfunctional family. Donald had a good heart but got upset easily. Many a quack emanated from him during moments of anger, befuddlement, or just general stress. Walt Disney comic books also featured the album concept, with, for example, Donald and his three nephews—Huey, Dewey, and Louie—viewing photographs that led them into recalling adventures involving not only themselves but also Daisy Duck, Uncle Scrooge, and Grandma Duck. In fact, there was a series of *Donald Duck Album* comic books.

Individual members of Donald's family enjoyed their own comic books as well, often around a theme, an approach that Dell Publishing seemed to favor in many of its comics. As readers were heading back to school at the end of summer, they—we—could commiserate with *Huey, Dewey and Louie Back to School*. Grandma Duck lived on a farm (where else?)—so the Duck family could have an appropriate grandmother's venue for adventures, escapades, and mild mischief. *Grandma Duck's Farm Friends* was another series, not just an isolated comic book.

Uncle Scrooge was a particular favorite of mine. As his name indicates, he was tight with a dollar but as susceptible to getting himself into trouble as any of his more spendthrift relatives. He was Donald's uncle, which technically made him a great-uncle to Donald's three nephews. His precise relationship to Grandma Duck never seemed entirely clear. Even less clear was the question of Huey, Dewey, and Louie's parents. Who they were I never ascertained. In fact, the relationship between Donald and Daisy always remained a bit vague as well. Daisy was sort of a girlfriend, although considerably more sophisticated and commonsensical than Donald. Needless to say, the relationship was thoroughly platonic. I think that the Walt Disney and Dell people wanted to keep any hint of sex out of all duck relationships, and equally out of mouse relationships.

That leads me to another set of Disney characters that I enjoyed for many years and through many dimes and quarters: Mickey Mouse, Minnie Mouse, and gang, including Goofy, the dog who was a friend of Mickey's. Mickey also had nephews—Morty and Ferdie—but they seemed to show up less often than Donald's three. Minnie was Mickey's girlfriend, although the relationship was no more physical than Donald and Daisy's. Like Daisy, she was very feminine.

Many other characters populated my comic books on occasion: Lassie, Tom Sawyer, Casper the Friendly Ghost, Disney's Shaggy Dog (from Disney's film world), the Lady and the Tramp (also from a film), and the puppy Scamp, among others.

A lot of my comic books have disappeared one way or another, but I retain many of them. Those that I have will stay. Excuse me while I take a short break for a little quality reading time.

4-H and Square Dancing

I was a member of 4-H, an organization popular with rural youngsters. As with most youth organizations, 4-H tried to combine education, development of proper values, and fun, the last being especially important if youngsters were to keep coming to meetings and participating in the organization's activities.

Building a sense of membership in a special group also is important for organizations, and 4-H tried (still tries) to do that. The organization has a pledge built around its four H's, which focus on the developmental goals and values of 4-H. The four H's, in the language found on the organization's web site, are:

Head—Managing, Thinking
Heart—Relating, Caring
Hands—Giving, Working
Health—Being, Living

The fourth one seems a little vague to me today, especially the "being" reference, which appears a bit too ontological for children. Nonetheless, it is hard to argue overall with the importance of these four elements.

From these values comes the pledge, which we would recite at the beginning of each meeting:

Edward J. Rielly

I pledge my head to clearer thinking,
My heart to greater loyalty,
My hands to larger service,
and my health to better living,
for my club, my community, my country, and my world.

Now following all of those promises is a tall order for a child as young as nine years of age. However, one cannot start too early at improving one's club, community, country, and world. The connections stated within the final part of the pledge convey the hope that what we did within our club, if extended in terms of the four basic values, would help us to improve our broader communities as we grew older.

One of the requirements was that we each complete an annual 4-H project. Normally, that project would be exhibited at the Lafayette County Fair, held in Darlington. I chose woodworking most of the time. Once, however, my project was a steer, but my steer, which I named Red because of its color (creativity not one of the four H's), contracted lockjaw, an inevitably fatal disease, and had to be put down. The event was mildly traumatic, although not as devastating for me as losing my dogs, a subject I talk about elsewhere in these pages. Whatever I made with wood—for example, a picnic table (a very heavy picnic table!)—ran little risk of developing a fatal disease and was a lot easier to take care of at the county fair. Wood requires little in the way of feeding, watering, and cleaning out its stall.

Each meeting was a combination of business and recreation. Meetings were held in those days in the Fayette Town Hall. Fayette was a small place, barely a village, in Fayette Township in Lafayette County. Our farm had the distinction of being partly in Fayette Township and partly in Willow Springs Township. Although the town line was to the east of our driveway a piece ("a piece" being a common rural unit of measurement without any set dimensions and never used in the plural, as in "six pieces"), our driveway was the meeting place, that is, the turning around location, for road graders in summer and snowplows in winter. My dad would drive me to the 4-H meetings and usually wait until the meeting was over. He could, of course, go home and return later if he wanted, as Fayette was just a few minutes from our farm.

I remember few details of specific meetings, but one form of entertainment stands out: the square dance. Being shy when I was young, especially around girls, I did not look forward to the dance. However, a square dance is a pretty conservative type of dance, requiring only a moderate amount of contact with members of the opposite sex—nothing like a slow waltz, where one is obliged to place an arm around the girl's waist while holding her other hand, while maintaining one's gaze more or less on the dance partner. The safety factor of the square dance (translated: keeping boys and girls reasonably far apart) no doubt figured into its selection by our adult club leaders.

Square dancing was especially popular among country folks and harkened back to the cowboy culture of the Old West. As the name implies, couples form a square and move through specific steps as someone calls the dance, that is, gives directions to the dancers. One might say that a square dance is, well, a "square" dance, fairly traditional and not what some people might consider hip or cool, especially those who want a lot of soulful gazing and closeness.

So when our entertainment for the evening was the square dance, I gritted my teeth and managed to participate, but I was always glad when the event ended and I could climb into our old Ford pickup and head home. Still, there was that one cute girl with the raven black hair who once in a while would end up as my partner. Maybe the experience was not all bad.

Learning About Death

There comes a time when every child learns about death—really learns about it. I'm not talking about having a pet die, even a dog that has grown into a close friend, which is a subject I talk about elsewhere. No, I mean having a person die—someone very close, someone you realize you will never see again, at least until we all make it to another, less fragile life.

That happened for me when I was eleven years old. My brother Lawrence, who was not quite twenty-seven yet, died. I refer to Lawrence several times elsewhere and briefly mention his death. He died in a river during a reunion of his wife's family and left behind two young boys, Tommy and Johnny.

Lawrence (although we usually called him Lawrencie, which, even as an adult, he did not take exception to, at least from us) was especially kind to young children, including his siblings. He was what a big brother should be and sometimes even is. My sister tells of how when she was a little girl, some boys who were friends of

Lawrence and I in a casual winter moment in our matching coats.

my brothers were playing in a small tent in our yard. Being boys, they would not let Mary enter the tent. Lawrence, also a boy but also a big brother, promptly put an end to that exclusionary practice by ordering the boys to vacate the premises in favor of Mary.

Even after Lawrence had married and moved to Rockford, Illinois, whenever he would return to the farm to visit us, he would always have time to play baseball with me. He would hit pop-ups to me, calling out, "Okay, Minnie, get that one!" or something to that effect. He knew, of course, that I was an ardent Chicago White Sox fan and a strong admirer of Minnie Minoso, Nellie Fox, and other White Sox heroes.

Although I have no vivid memory of it, photographs clearly show that Lawrence and I had identical coats, except, of course, for size. They consisted of black and white squares. I wish that I recalled the circumstances behind our getting them. The symbolism, though, is obvious (the closeness that Lawrence and I felt toward each other) and certainly validates the memories of Lawrence that do remain with me.

So it was an awful night when we received word that Lawrence was missing in the Pecatonica River near Calamine, Wisconsin. The call came from my Aunt Katy, who had been asked (by whom I cannot remember) to contact us. Some Chicago cousins were visiting at the time, and one,

Mary Eileen Gavagan, who was older than I, was left in charge of the younger children while Mom, Dad, and my older siblings rushed to the river. As I mention at another place in this memoir, Father Doyle, our pastor, joined them at the river and stayed, faithfully supplying much needed support. Finally, divers found Lawrence, but it was far too late.

Meanwhile, I was left at home. It is strange how certain images remain with one, even small details that have no special significance except that they occupy that moment. I recall doing dishes with my older cousin, an effort on her part, I believe, to keep my mind off what was occurring at the river. It was a hot summer's day—July 3—and the window was open over the sink. I remember flies landing on the dishes, black specks against white plates. That image of flies remains vivid. Maybe it also is a symbol, but I will leave that matter to others.

It was a very hard time for my parents as well as for the rest of us in my family—and obviously for Lawrence's wife, Ruth, and their sons. It is strange that I cannot remember precisely what I felt then. No doubt a psychologist could explain why—perhaps something about repressing terrible sorrow—but I have felt enough loss over my brother in later years, I think, to make up for that suppression. And, having spent many years by now as a parent and grandparent, I still can only imagine (fortunately) what it must have been like for my parents. It is a common saying that the worst experience for parents is losing a child. Common sayings, as we all know, sometimes are one hundred percent correct.

So I learned about death that year in my childhood. I have learned a lot more about it through experience since, but that was my first moment of true, colossal loss.

VI.
My Hometown

Which Town is This?

Our farm was eight miles from the town of Mineral Point and twelve miles from Darlington. Although farther away, Darlington was our official hometown. We went to church there, did the bulk of our shopping in the town, and each of us children went to high school in Darlington. Still, we went to Mineral Point often enough, especially as it was a bit closer. The two towns were in different directions from our farm. We went south to Darlington and northwest to Mineral Point. So because they were about the same size, roughly two thousand strong, distinguishing between them should have been easy.

And so it became—once I put on a few years. But when I was very young, I needed a point of reference, a defining difference, to know where I was. Everybody needs those points of reference, of course, and I still do, though for perhaps more weighty reasons than figuring out which small town I am in.

For me, the difference in those days was the dog. It was a black dog, high above me on a platform jutting out from the second story of a store on the right-hand side as we drove up the hill that constituted the main street of Mineral Point. The dog was a pointer—no surprise there. It stood straight and true, its legs rigid, its tail curving upward in a slight arc, its head alert, nose pointing to some invisible, omnipresent duck or goose in the sky.

And it shone, jet black, as our pickup climbed the hill, my dad shifting down to make the grade, his feet pumping the clutch and brake, switching onto and off the accelerator flawlessly.

Maybe I should have known which town I was in from the steep crawl up the main drag in Mineral Point, but I always needed that dog to be sure. There's that dog. This is Mineral Point.

A few years ago, I got to wondering about that dog. Because of the way just about everything changes, I wondered if it were still there, still pointing to some high-flying birds. So I made sure when we were back visiting to take a drive to Mineral Point. As I climbed the hill in my easy automatic, I looked up and to the right.

Edward J. Rielly

Sure enough! The dog was still there, still pointing faithfully. But it had changed. The glistening black had turned to gray after all these years, something to which many of us can relate. I hated to see that, though, and wished the town leaders might have taken better care of him. Such faithfulness deserves some reward.

Bottles of Pop

It's called soda in the East where I live now, but in the Midwest people always called it pop. Remember the old joke kids loved to throw around? "I don't drink anything stronger than pop, but, boy, can Pop drink some strong stuff."

Those were the good, simple days when pop was pop. No diet pop, no caffeine-free pop, just regular, full-strength pop. Stores and gas stations had those boxy coolers with bottles of various flavors standing in water. You would just reach in, your hand submerged in ice-cold water, and pull out the flavor you wanted. On the side of the cooler was a bottle opener because, of course, pop did not come in cans or in bottles with lids that screwed off.

One of the thrills of my childhood was going with my dad to the pop factory in town. Its official name was the Badger State Mineral Water Company. The building was built over a spring that supplied pure, glistening water that in turn produced other wonderful liquids. We would buy a case of pop, and I would get to pick the flavors, choosing carefully as if I were plucking diamonds glittering on green grass.

I always chose several bottles of strawberry, some grape and orange, and a few cream sodas. Such fun, choosing those flavors. It was a world awash in pop! I think that I enjoyed the choosing more than the drinking.

My dad (never once in my entire life did I call him "Pop") and I would haul the case home in the back of our pickup. We might drive a car to Sunday church but never to carry out those serious manly roles, like buying pop.

Have you noticed how hard it is to get a good bottle of strawberry pop these days?

The Fair Store

One of the most exciting reasons for going to Darlington was visiting the Fair Store. That name was conjured up by a gentleman in Chicago way back in 1874, when he opened a discount department store that promised to be like a fair, a place where folks could find lots of items for reasonable costs and have a lot of fun doing it, like visiting booths at a county fair. Of course, the name also implied that those low costs were designed to be fair to people of moderate means, giving a good product for a modest price.

I cannot remember when the name of the store was actually changed. At some point it became the S. S. Kresge store. However, whatever name was on the front, the store always remained the Fair Store to us. I really did not focus on its being fair, or even like a county fair, since those marketing strategies were way over my head. But I did find it a lot of fun to visit. One could find just about anything there: candy, clothes, pots and pans, greeting cards, toys, and on and on.

What most excited me was the candy. Just inside the door was a set of glass containers holding loose candy. You could buy as much as you wanted or had the money for. My dad liked a maple candy that is still available today, usually, of course, in already packed and sealed bags. My preferences were chocolate. I especially loved chocolate stars and bridge mix. What pleasure it was to go in and say, "Please give me a quarter pound of chocolate stars." It did not take much money to buy candy then, although even a little bit of money was important to my family, who never had a lot to waste.

I also could buy my packages of baseball cards and gum at the Fair Store. I bought a lot of them over the years.

Then there were the toys. By today's standards, formed from huge toy stores, the offerings were indeed moderate. However, so was the price. It was a great place to buy plastic soldiers and such.

One of my most vivid memories of the Fair Store is of my parents buying an Easter basket with artificial green grass and lots of candy, including marshmallow rabbits and jelly beans, the whole package wrapped in cellophane paper. I cannot recall much of what my mother bought there. I was too busy looking at the toys and candy, but she shopped at the store quite a bit. Maybe she did find it a fair place to shop.

A Place Called Wanderscheid's

One of the stores we most often frequented in our hometown of Darlington during my childhood was Wanderscheid's Grocery Store. To people who shop at today's large supermarkets, it would not seem like much of a grocery store. Probably one aisle of a typical supermarket would surpass all of Wanderscheid's in square feet. It was neither the only grocery store in town, nor even the largest. Yet it was the one we went to most often.

I'm not sure how to explain our preference for Wanderscheid's. I recall no comments by my mother, who did virtually all of our grocery shopping there, about its prices being lower than in other grocery stores in town. It was, however, a store that fostered a strong sense of familiarity. I can recall only three people working at the store, although others may have filled in at times: the owner after whom the store was named, his wife, and another man who generally would be found behind the meat counter.

There was one aisle in the store. It formed a circle, with customers typically turning right after entering and following the aisle to the far end of the store, where the meat counter stood. Buying meat therefore usually occurred halfway through the shopping. Behind the meat counter was the storeroom, a mysterious, shadowy room into which I, of course, never ventured.

After buying our meat, we continued down the other side of the store toward the checkout counter, completing our circular path. Mr. Wanderscheid or his wife usually would be there to ring up our purchases. She was quiet; he was not. The proprietor usually had something humorous to say. After I wore a pink shirt one day, he referred to me a number of times during subsequent visits as Clark, alluding to the then-famous actor Clark Gable. Gable was handsome, debonair, and a genuine heartthrob (a term applied in those days to a man who made ladies' hearts beat faster). I was, I admit, not much possessed of those qualities, even if Mr. Wanderscheid saw some connection between my pink shirt and the actor.

In the corner of the store, across from where we would pay for our groceries and a bit to the left, just inside the large plate-glass window, stood the pop cooler. The cooler was much like the milk cooler we had on our farm, though much smaller. It contained ice-cold water, and the bottles stood in the water, their necks rising above the surface. That icy pop made for a refreshing drink on a hot day. A cold hand from ferreting out the desired flavor felt good, too.

I often accompanied my mother on her shopping trips while Dad waited in our pickup. He was the chauffeur because Mom did not drive. The bags of groceries went into the box of the pickup. The twelve-mile drive home could raise havoc on a summer day with ice cream and such; on a cold winter's day, a lot more food might be frozen than we wanted. A rainy day called for some feed sacks or other covering. The trip home did not help the food much, but on the other hand it did not do irreparable harm either. We lived with the consequences of dwelling far out in the country.

Two specific dimensions to my relationship with Wanderscheid's store still merit some attention. The first may appear rather odd; in fact, it strikes me that way a bit now, but I guess that everyone's childhood has its oddities. I actually enjoyed those shopping trips, so much so that once in a great while I, in consultation with my mother, did the shopping. She would accompany me, but I made some decisions and also paid for the groceries. That may seem especially weird for a child—not only paying for the groceries, but actually wanting to do it—but that was my attitude. Mr. Wanderscheid commented, in words that I remember precisely, "You can never start too young." Of course, he was hardly a disinterested bystander. My mother, however, directed me away from paying on a regular basis because she obviously knew that I did not have a lot of personal money.

Edward J. Rielly

I think that what especially appealed to me was to some extent being in charge. As I look back I think that my mother, who never took a psychology class in her life, understood that growing up involves asserting some control, acquiring a little power; and even if that control is exercised in a somewhat strange way—say buying groceries—so long as it is not directed toward something bad it should be allowed, even encouraged, within limits.

The other significant memory I have of Wanderscheid's is stopping down there during lunch hour when I was in high school. I often ate in the basement of the Catholic Church across the street from the high school, which served as the school's cafeteria. At times, though, I longed to forget about those little, thin strips of paper that served as lunch tickets, which we turned in as we entered to Otto Ruf, who along with teaching physics and coaching football and baseball, was the ticket collector. The routine of lunch grew tedious without an occasional break from cafeteria food. So sometimes I would visit Wanderscheid's, just a couple of blocks downtown from the high school. Quite a few of us did that. We were a pretty well-behaved bunch, and a lot of our parents shopped there, so the proprietor did not mind our visits, even when we ate our lunch leaning against the pop cooler. After all, why should he? What we ate we had just bought from him. A couple pieces of cold meat, a bottle of pop, something sweet like a Hostess cupcake, and we were set for afternoon classes and football practice.

It's funny, but I especially remember the cold meat. My favorite was what was called Old-Fashioned loaf. I never find that particular type of cold meat anymore, which is too bad because I would like to see if it would still taste as good as I remember.

The building remains, but the store is long gone. The building, however, is still referred to by many people by the name of that seller of groceries: the Wanderscheid Grocery Building.

Main Street

The Fair Store and Wanderscheid's Grocery were not the only stores on Darlington's Main Street (or on nearby side streets) that mattered to me when I was growing up. In fact, there were quite a few stores that remain in my memory, still loaded with whatever drew my family and me into them in the days long gone by. To my mind, the Fair Store had no real competition as my favorite, but there were other stores that ranked high.

One of the unusual aspects of Main Street was the presence of several grocery stores, considering that Darlington was a town of little more than two thousand souls. We sometimes shopped at the A & P Store, approximately half way down Main Street on the left. It was larger than Wanderscheid's and therefore contained more options, but it lacked the intimacy of its smaller competitor from up the street. We also had a Kroger's, but for some reason we seldom went there. Maybe because it was even farther downtown. All of the grocery stores, for some reason, aligned themselves on the left side as one drove from the top of the street down toward the Pecatonica River.

Below Wanderscheid's but above the others was a strange building that passed for a grocery store, but also seemed to fall into the category of a general store. It appeared to have whatever the owner had accumulated over the years and never sold. The Schreiter Grocery Store was operated, not surprisingly, by a Mr. Schreiter, the descendant of at least a couple of earlier Mr. Schreiters who had operated out of the building. The store stood on a corner and had an imposing corner entrance up a flight of steps. I seldom entered the store but had the impression of darkness, dustiness, and items that, I imagined, had been sitting on those shelves for many a year. There seldom appeared to be much business, but some older men would gather there to talk. I may, of course, be doing Mr. Schreiter a serious injustice here, but I could only rely on my impressionable, youthful perceptions, and they convinced me that seldom did an object pass from a dusty shelf into the hands of a buyer (the term *consumer* being largely unknown then).

Edward J. Rielly

A few other stores (still on the left) figured prominently in our lives. Berk's sold clothes, one of two establishments offering the full run of clothing, including suits. Compared to the large stores that today offer clothing, selections were certainly limited but nonetheless sufficient. The other clothing store, DeMuth's, was across the street. We shopped there more often. Shoes were available at the McGreane Shoe Store, and we regularly bought our family shoes there.

Variety was the name of the game at several stores: the Fair Store, Schreiter's, and, perhaps most of all, an establishment run by Phil Weigel. Charlie Sleep, a longtime Darlington pharmacist, in retirement expanded his study of local history and reported his findings in an extraordinary series of "Sleepwalking" essays in the local paper, the *Republican Journal*. Mr. Sleep notes that Mr. Weigel's store just about defied placement in any category, as he "sold nearly anything that was saleable." How true!

Mr. Weigel sold toys, clothes, on and on. One item, however, stands out: a toy train. My mother decided to buy a toy train for me for one Christmas. (Or perhaps it was a birthday gift. Having been born on December 22, I celebrated two gift-receiving events three days apart, making it hard to keep straight the occasion for specific presents.) It was a simple train, only a few cars long—neither electric nor especially fancy. She did not have the money for it when she first spotted the train, but the proprietor put it aside for her. When my mother accumulated the required sum, she picked it up. So for me, Phil Weigel's store will always be the train store.

When I needed a haircut, I usually visited Joe McCarten's barbershop. Elsewhere I talk about my first haircut, but after that traumatic event I learned to take haircuts as a normal part of life. McCarten's establishment was an old-time barbershop for an old-time time. A large ledge inside the big window facing Main Street was littered with magazines and newspapers, and a row of chairs lined the wall facing the barber chair. If I were unlucky, I had to spend a considerable amount of time in one of those chairs waiting my turn. Mr. McCarten was rather old then, and for that reason I continue to picture barbers as senior citizens, even now that I have had my hair cut not only by young men but also by young women. Reality has a hard time pushing fixed perceptions aside.

In those days, a barber's prime tools were a scissors and comb. However, he also made skilled use of a long straight razor during haircuts as well as for men who came in for a shave. Some men still did that when I was young. The razor's role in a haircut was to shave the back and sides of the neck. I can still feel the tickle of the blade sliding down my neck. It obviously was very sharp, the leather strap that the barber used to sharpen it hanging beside the barber chair. The technical name for the strap was a strop. Perhaps it was the vowel change that gave the strop its special sharpening ability.

The pool hall, run by Dick Hastert, was one of the spots where people could get some enjoyable nonalcoholic refreshments. My father did not play pool, but he liked to stop in and have a malted milk. I never developed a taste for it myself, preferring, whenever I accompanied Dad into the pool hall, a glass of Coke or perhaps a cherry phosphate, which was an especially fizzy carbonated drink made with acid phosphate. Across the street and down a bit was the Sweet Shop, a soda fountain type of place where local youths gathered in the evening. I seldom made it into the Sweet Shop, though, because I was gathering instead with sheep and cows instead of classmates in the evening.

Also on the right side of the street was Muldoon's Bakery. I longed for the huge plain doughnuts that were sold there. They may not have been quite as large as I remember, since much seems big to a child, but they were light and really good, although not in the same class with my mother's frycakes. The other bakery item that stands out in my memory came from a bakery in Mineral Point: saffron buns. I enjoyed the taste, but the unusual color for buns—yellow—might have made them seem tastier than they actually were. If anyone still uses saffron in baking, I have not noticed for some five decades.

Leo Donahoe's Mobil Station was situated on the right fairly far up Main Street, so it was convenient for pulling in to buy gas as we arrived in town. Leo was almost always there, pumping gas and working on cars. He did a lot of basic maintenance, such as tune-ups and oil changes. The place was small, but he was reliable and always friendly. It often was our first stop. Here I will make it my last.

Darlington had just about everything we needed to buy in those

Edward J. Rielly

days, and just about every service that we needed, including doctors, dentists, banks, lumber yards, lockers (for frozen meat), drug stores ("pharmacies" they are called now), a pop factory, and more. Except for Mineral Point, we seldom went anywhere else to shop, certainly not to Dubuque or Madison, as those trips would take much of the day, and we seldom had that much time. Milking and other chores always awaited us on the farm.

Main Street has changed a lot since then. The businesses that I mention have receded into the past, so anyone searching for them today would search in vain. However, in my memory the street still runs the same, the same businesses still lining it all the way to the bridge spanning the Pecatonica.

The County Fair

The Lafayette County Fair was an annual highlight, a few days of gaudy colors, bright lights, men with tattoos on their arms summoning young and old alike to spend their money, animal-filled barns, rides that went high and fast, and greasy food that delighted a child's taste buds. Actually, a great deal regarding the county fair delighted me. Whether that was because of a child's lack of discerning taste or because of an extraordinary capacity for wonder remains in doubt these many years later. What is not in doubt is that I had a great time every summer at the fair.

The county fair even had its academic component. We prepared school entries, as did kids from most of the surrounding schools. The leaf collection was an old standby. Find a Wisconsin native who was a child in the 1940s or '50s and had never put together a leaf collection, and I will show you someone who must have spent an entire childhood asleep.

Of course, we made displays out of wood, cardboard, paper, just about any substance that could be written on, nailed together, pasted, glued, colored, or taped: science displays, veritable zoos of animals, diagrams of how engines worked. Creativity blossomed in preparation for the fair. And then we waited for the ribbons. Any ribbon was tolerable, but the blue ribbon was what we really aspired to. Entering the academic display building and seeing that blue ribbon filled me with pride.

A lot of farm kids also took animals to the fair. I never did that, despite being in 4-H. Bunking in an open shed among bales of straw and hay, a heady mixture of cow, sheep, and pig odors, and uncertain weather that could swing from 100-plus degrees to roaring thunderstorms, all to make sure that one's animal was taken care of throughout the day and night, did not seem like something even then that would quite make my day.

Even more exciting than blue ribbons, though, was the midway, that dusty path down through booths and rides that seemed created from a child's dream. Here I could dip plastic fish out of a rectangular pond to win a prize corresponding to the number on the bottom of the duck; there I could exercise my thin right pitching arm to knock down bottles that seemed so reluctant to tip even when the ball gave them a good lick; and just beyond I could fling darts at balloons. The rows of prizes proved as alluring as a Siren's call, and I plunked down my quarters with great optimism.

Of course, the largest, most enticing objects usually remained on their shelves, and I went away with a small consolation prize that neither consoled me then nor deterred me from trying again the following year.

I did not like heights so I avoided the Ferris Wheel. Speed, though, was good, so long as I remained close to the ground, as I did in the Tilt-a-Whirl, a metal half-circle that whirled around and around, sometimes making a full arc, other times going only so far before swinging madly back. I clutched the safety bar and held on as I jolted right and left. I recall a somewhat similar ride that consisted of what essentially were square boxes at the end of metal beams. The boxes whipped side to side, always threatening to smash into other boxes, but never quite hitting them. The name of that particular ride escapes me now, but not the excitement of it. Bumper cars were fun, too. They actually looked like cars, and we could collide with each other—actually more of a gentle bumping. That may not seem like great training for future driving since the goal was to collide, but we did not have a lot of future-think at the time.

There were many children's rides that I think adults would have continued to enjoy but felt embarrassed to ride. The carousel was one. I suspect that those adults riding it alongside their young children were happy for an acceptable excuse to mount one of the galloping wooden horses, much as I enjoyed doing decades later with a child or grandchild in tow.

A hamburger or hot dog naturally tasted much better at the fair than at home. The real culinary delights, however, those that I never got at home, were cotton candy and snow cones. The common denominator between the two was stickiness: the sticky pink fluff of cotton candy on my fingers, the sticky purple syrup of the snow cone dripping through the paper container. But how sweet both were!

Then there was the tent with lots of machines into which I could put money and out of which I could extract various fragile treasures. One such type of machine particularly attracted me: the picture-dispensing machines, especially the one that dispensed baseball pictures. I inserted coins (how many I no longer recall) and out came a picture, much larger than the baseball cards packaged with gum, about five and a half by three and a half inches. A Stan Musial. A Ralph Kiner. A Robin Roberts. Once when I was gathering in these baseball cards, I ran out of coins. I tracked down my father, who at the time was talking with friends, and asked if I could have more money. Asking for money was something I seldom did, but, after all, we are talking about baseball pictures here. Maybe Nellie Fox was residing inside the machine just waiting for me. Dad gave me some money, and I returned to the machines.

There was another machine that dispensed pictures of Western film and television stars. I still have those Western pictures as well. Hugh O'Brian hoists a shotgun in case the star on his chest fails to deter evildoers. Richard Boone smiles, as if to put me at ease, exhibiting neither a gun nor his calling card: "Have Gun Will Travel." Dick Powell scowls, Dale Robertson smirks, and Roy Rogers lovingly adjusts the collar of his wife, Dale Evans.

Another county fair staple is the sideshow, a tent in which one can view all kinds of unusual creatures, human and otherwise. The sideshow used to be known rather unkindly as a "freak show." Such tents did not attract me, probably because of some combination of parental commands and my own personal skepticism. I preferred instead the rides, the cotton candy, the modest prizes, baseball pictures, and an occasional blue ribbon.

Cemeteries

Visiting cemeteries is not an enticing way to spend time when a person is young—or old, for that matter. Nor was it for me. But I did it quite a bit, not necessarily with enthusiasm, more as just acquiescing to a standard family tradition. My family was hardly unique in visiting where family members are buried, but we may have been inclined to do it more often than most. We frequented cemeteries for the usual reasons—to plant flowers on graves and pray for the deceased—but also out of an interest in our family history and because of a special relationship to the small country graveyard not far from our farm.

Three cemeteries were especially relevant to our interests, all of them nearby in southwestern Wisconsin: Holy Rosary Cemetery in Darlington; Immaculate Conception Cemetery in Truman; and Holy Assumption Cemetery in Willow Springs Township. As the names imply, all are Catholic cemeteries.

Most of my mother's ancestors are buried in the Truman cemetery. It resides out in the country, is still used today, and continues to be nicely maintained. My mother's parents, James McKeon and Julia (Fox) McKeon, are buried there, as are most of my mother's siblings, including Mary (McKeon) Johnson, with whom my mother was very close, no doubt partly because she was the sibling closest in age to my mother, who was the youngest in the family. Unfortunately, Mary died very young, at the age of twenty-nine in 1928. Also buried at Truman is my Aunt Katie, Mom's sibling I knew best. She was famous for the sugar cookies I talk about elsewhere in this memoir.

Our journeys to the Immaculate Conception Cemetery occurred at relatives' funerals or whenever my mother just wanted to visit family graves. Her mother died in 1939, so I never knew her; Mom's father, who died at the age of ninety-seven in 1955, I remember as a somewhat distant and obviously very old man. A list of those buried in the cemetery, which was established in 1856, was printed and distributed a few years ago. Most of the names (Boyle, Bradley, Donahoe, Doyle, Fox, Kliebenstein, McDermot, McDonald, McKeon, Mulcahy, to name just a few examples) include relatives of ours by descent or marriage

Holy Rosary Cemetery we visited often. Some relatives of Dad's were buried there, including Father Michael McQuaid, Dad's uncle, who was a brother to his mother, Catherine (McQuaid) Rielly. Father McQuaid, who as a priest occupied an important place in our roster of relatives, died in 1949 on December 12, ten days before my sixth birthday. I have absolutely no memory of him at all.

When the first child in my family, Bernard, or Bernie as we called him, died as an infant in 1927, slightly more than a month after his birth, he was buried in Holy Rosary. Of course, we visited his grave many times. My parents had purchased lots in the cemetery, and Bernie, whose death was very traumatic for my parents, was placed there, awaiting his parents. My mother told of how my father cried and cried at his death. I cannot recall ever seeing my father cry, despite his being a very gentle, loving, and supportive father.

After their deaths, Dad's in 1972 and Mom's in 1992, my parents were buried in Holy Rosary with Bernie.

In some ways, however, my family was most involved in Holy Assumption Cemetery. It was, and still is, pretty isolated, surrounded by cornfields and pastures. The church that once stood in its midst is long gone. Our farm was a few miles to the northeast but seemed only a few hills away. The most recent graves held relatives of ours on Dad's side, including his parents. My grandfather, Edward Rielly, had been buried there in 1950, alongside his wife, Catherine, who died terribly prematurely, at thirty-one in 1912, leaving eight children.

In 1955, my brother Robert Lawrence Rielly died by drowning at a picnic gathering of his wife's family, a loss that I detailed earlier.

Lawrence was a few weeks from his twenty-seventh birthday and left behind two young sons. His wife decided to have Lawrence buried in Holy Assumption because she wanted him to be close to his ancestors.

That decision was one that my mother later agonized over many times, wondering if Lawrence also should have been buried in Darlington. Already Holy Assumption had become almost a personal family cemetery. Many buried there, of course, were not relatives of ours, although a large number of the families came from County Monaghan in Ireland, as did the Riellys. We did not know at the time that Lawrence would be the final person laid to rest in the cemetery, as our grandfather had been buried there only a few years earlier.

The cemetery eventually became deactivated, and responsibility for its upkeep would become uncertain. For years, we did most of the work at the cemetery: mowing grass, planting flowers, clearing away brush, maintaining the fence and gate, and keeping a steady eye on the place in case of vandalism or some other problem such as cattle wandering in.

My remaining brother, Joseph Francis, who passed away in 1996, did a lot of work at Holy Assumption and was deeply interested in the history that it contained. Gradually, indeed, the cemetery came to feel like ours.

That sense remained, even after both of my parents and Joe died and were buried in the Darlington cemetery. My sister, Mary (Rielly) Flanagan, continued to keep careful track of cemetery conditions and visited it regularly, even after the township of Willow Springs took over its maintenance. My wife, children, and I would visit it on each trip back to Wisconsin, and each time the cemetery and the farm, although no longer ours, seemed close enough so that we could almost reach out from one and touch the other.

Many people do not visit cemeteries. Maybe they are right, for the real self does not reside there. Still, cemeteries are too deeply fixed in my background and in my sense of family not to keep going back. That returning seems to be like my whole childhood. I just keep going back.

Edward J. Rielly

The End